PRISON SLANG

This book is for my wife Shari
who has had to carry the burden,
but knows the best years are still to come.
My children Shannon, Michelle and Willy
who taught me to see the sunshine
and how to smile again.
My mother
who raised me as a child
and raised me from the ashes as an adult.
The memory of my father
who knows I'm back on my feet.
My sister
who is always a friend.

WKB

To the memory of:
My mother Mary, and my step-father Ben.
My wife Kathy—
My future past—always loved and remembered.
They made my life special.

My sons, Matt and Josh.
My love, Yvonne
My future.
They make life worth living again.

JMC

Prison Slang

Words and Expressions
Depicting Life Behind Bars

by

William K. Bentley

and

James M. Corbett

McFarland & Company, Inc., Publishers
Jefferson, North Carolina, and London

British Library Cataloguing-in-Publication data available

Library of Congress Cataloguing-in-Publication data available

Library of Congress Catalog Card Number 91-52763

ISBN 0-89950-646-1 (lib. bdg.; 55# acid-free natural paper) ∞

Manufactured in the United States of America

McFarland & Company, Inc., Publishers
  Box 611, Jefferson, North Carolina 28640

TABLE OF CONTENTS

v

ACKNOWLEDGMENTS

Like any project this book could not have been done by any single individual. Countless hours of brainstorming and discussion were lovingly donated to the creation of this work.

We would like to thank: Nancy Reed for all of her efforts and for making the Rio Salado Community College chemical dependency program at the prison a life changing experience; Carol Scarafiotti for providing the leadership and direction for allowing people to grow and for bringing the chemical dependency program to the "inside"; Dr. Charles Landis of Tolleson Union High School for always being a mentor and friend.

Without the help and expertise of Fred Hill we would have never finished the book. I can't say thank you too many times, especially for all of those early, early mornings. Dr. Donald Damstra and Dr. William Calderwood have shown me what the words empathy and recovery really mean. You always had faith in the project. Dr. William Phillips showed me that the book had potential and helped in giving the book direction.

The following people made significant contributions and we wish to thank them:

Gilbert Lucero   Donna Mobley
Donald Peyton   Mitzi Schireman

A special thanks to the members of the "brain-trust":

Hank Gatens   Danny Wilson
Kent Brown   Richard "Frizz" Sauter

Prison Slang

Fred Van Haelst   Adrian Le Chance
Dan Chance   Rick Pina
Teddy O'Sullivan   Chance Stewart
Phillip Beck

INTRODUCTION

Prison Slang is composed of words and expressions used in prison. They are divided into categories based on the major aspects of prison existence. By examining these words, the reader will see into a way of life not normally seen by "outsiders." It is a way of life nobody should want to experience.

While these expressions are used in prison, this is not to say many of them will not be familiar to some individuals as "street" vernacular. Language is mobile and does not respect the confines of prison walls. Even if some of the words are familiar, it should be noted that these are words used extensively in prison and make up the vocabulary of this way of life. They are, therefore, important in creating a portrait of that life.

The authors believe language is a reflection of life. Words are created and used to portray and express conditions and lifestyles. What better glimpse into the life of the incarcerated can a person get than to study the language of the inmate? Why study or discuss this way of life? Who cares about criminals and what they do? If taken in a vacuum, no one would care, but the law reaches out and touches everyone. This is not a book written about the plight of the inmate. Rather, it is a glimpse into a way of life through its own words which instills an image for the reader that will cause some degree of inner reflection.

The words of the various chapters are grouped by topic, arranged alphabetically under each subheading. This creates a continuity of thought and helps the reader better understand the content. An alphabetical listing of all words is in the index.

Language is not static but is instead constantly changing. Prison jargon is no exception. Many of the words used today have counterparts found in times past. When applicable, these words are indicated following the appropriate entry. These words may still be used by a few "old timers," but they are not used by the majority of the prison population.

William K. Bentley was recently released after serving five years in Arizona State Prison for burglary, while James M. Corbett served five years in Indiana State Prison and five years in Arizona State Prison for armed robbery. We have served time. Spend some time taking an insider's look at a way of life hidden from most people, a way of life no one should have to endure.

1

INSTITUTIONALIZATION

Prisons

Band Box A county workhouse or prison.

Big House Prison.

Calaboose Antiquated expression for jail or prison.

Camp A relatively small prison, usually set in a rural location. A camp can be a work camp, with inmates being used for local labor, an honor camp housing minimum security inmates, or a small rural prison.

Can A jail or prison. (Archaic: *piss-can*)

Cannery A prison.

Clink An old expression for a county jail or a state prison. It is still used by some convicts.

Concrete Womb An antiquated term for prison.

Coop A prison.

County Hotel A county jail or workhouse.

Crossbar Hotel A humorous name for prison or jail. The name comes from the presence of steel bars in prison cells. (Archaic: *jug, canister*)

Disneyland An easy prison in which to do time. (Archaic: *playhouse*)

General Population In prison society, most prisoners are afforded a certain degree of freedom. They are allowed to work, attend schools and utilize the recreation area. These inmates are known as the general population and constitute the majority of the prisoners. Some inmates who are not in general population are ones who are in protective segregation or lockup units and death row inmates.

Gladiator School Every prison system has a gladiator school. This is the name given the prison where the young trouble-makers are sent. These inmates are generally 18 to 25 years old and have that "I don't give a damn" attitude. Gladiator schools breed gang members because fighting and criminal activities are the primary lessons learned there. (Archaic: *kindergarten*)

Guard Hall The area of a prison where the prison guards receive their instructions. The guard hall is used for the guards' roll call, shift instructions and other security matters.

Hen Pen A prison for women.

Iron House A prison.

Iron Pile *also* **Weight Pile** The area of the recreation yard of a prison where weightlifting equipment is kept and used.

Joint The most popular and widely used term referring to prison. "He is back in the joint for armed robbery." (Archaic: *college*)

Kimona A prison coffin, usually just a pine box.

Marble Orchard *also* **Gallery 13** Most maximum security prisons housing inmates who are doing long sentences have their own cemeteries. Such a cemetery is known as the Marble Orchard or Gallery 13. Inmates who die in prison and are not claimed by relatives or friends are buried there.

Pen A seldom used word meaning prison. Inmates often feel as if they are caged or penned like animals, thus they sometimes refer to prison in this manner. (Archaic: *lag, limbo*)

Poogie A prison.

School of Crime *also* **Campus** Prison. Many young and inexperienced inmates can learn about crime and how to commit crimes here.

Slammer Anyone who has never been confined in prison can not fully comprehend the haunting reality of a steel cell door slamming shut each night. As you lie in your two by six foot bed, that slamming sound echoes in your mind throughout the night. The slammer is a term that means prison and is derived from this relentless and tormenting slamming of the cell doors. (Archaic: *big house*)

Stir An old term that means prison. "He has to serve another ten years in stir." (Archaic: *states*)

Stone Dump A prison.

The Walls *also* **Behind the Walls** Almost every maximum security prison has a concrete or brick wall, ranging in height from 25 to 40 feet surrounding the prison grounds. These prisons are known as the walls. Inmates in these institutions are referred to as being in the walls or behind the walls. (Archaic: *Bastille*)

Yard The recreation area of a prison. Most prisons are designed to have housing, work and recreation areas.
      In some prisons, however, the entire area to which inmates have access is referred to as the yard.

Cells

Alley The corridor in front of a row of cells or between rows of cells.

Boxcar A prison cell.

Bug Trap A steel cot or bed in a prison cell.

Bull Pen *also* **Cage** *and* **Holding Cell** Waiting areas. These areas are used to hold inmates waiting to be processed into the prison or medical or court returns. These holding cells are steel mesh or steel bar cages.

Can Any place used to confine prisoners. The term is used to mean jail, prison or a prison cell. (Archaic: *pokey, pogey, coffin*)

Catwalk Any walking area in a cellhouse, primarily the walking area in front of the cells. Originally, the term catwalk was used to mean the walking areas the prison guards used for their observation of the cells. These catwalks were manned by armed guards and only the guards had access to these areas. In recent years, catwalk has expanded to mean any walking area in a cellhouse, especially the walking areas in front of the cells that are on the upper levels.

Cement Tomb A prison cell.

Double Bunking Putting two men in the same cell. This is not merely a practice where inmates share a cell, but it usually refers to a practice of putting two men in a cell that was made for one person. This is done in prisons where there is a severe overcrowding problem.

　　The practice of double bunking leads to a great deal of tension amongst the prison population, and there is usually a correlative rise in violence.

Drum A prison cell. (Archaic: *shebang*)

8-8-16 A concrete block prison cell. This stands for $8'' \times 8'' \times 16''$. These are the dimensions of a concrete construction block. (Archaic: *hut*)

Eyes Hand mirrors used by inmates to look down their row of cells. Since all cells are only open to the front, it is impossible to look down the run without eyes. Inmates hold these mirrors out through the bars of their cells and position them so they can see in any direction.

Fart Sack A general reference to one's bed. Also can refer to a cotton mattress cover that fits completely over a mattress and is drawn tight with pull strings. (Archaic: *pad, kip*)

Flag The bottom or ground floor row of cells in a cellhouse. "His cell is on the flag." (Archaic: *flats*)

Grill *also* **Cell Grill** The barred or steel mesh front of a cell. (Archaic: *slats*)

House An inmate's prison cell. This is one of the most important aspects of prison life as a person's house is his home, his solitude, where he achieves his privacy. Here, he may be able to lend some individualism to his gloomy existence. An inmate's house is his living area where his bed and personal property are kept. (Archaic: *den, pad*)

Hut A prison cell.

Judas *also* **Judas Slit** In some prisons, the cell doors are made of solid steel instead of steel bars. In these solid steel doors there is a slit or peephole that enables the guards to observe the inmates. This peephole is called a "Judas Slit" or a "Judas."

Junk Tank Prison cells reserved exclusively for drug addicts or alcoholics.

Rackin' the Bars *also* **Rackin' the Doors** The opening or closing of the cell doors. "They rack the bars every morning at 6 A.M. for breakfast."

Range A row of cells in a cellhouse. "Daryl's cell is on C range."

Rollin' the Bars The manner in which cell doors are opened. In many prisons, the cell doors on each row of cells are opened and closed automatically at specific times. The cell doors are made of steel bars and operate on steel rollers that are connected so they open or close simultaneously. This is known as rollin' the bars. (Archaic: *slam the slats*)

Run A row of prison cells in a cellhouse. "His cell is all the way up on the top run." A run can be the walking area in front of the cells or both the cells and the walking area.

Tier A row of cells in a cellhouse. Tier is used primarily to indicate the rows of cells that are stacked atop of one another. "Daryl's cell is on the third tier." Tier is also used to indicate the entire area of a row of cells including the walking area in front of the cells.

Tiger Cage Some prisons have underground security sections that house inmates. A prison cell located in one of these underground sections is known as a tiger cage.

Walk The route a prison guard uses as he periodically checks the area to which he is assigned. "The guard is making his walk now."
Another usage for a walk is any walking area in front of or inside a cellhouse. In a prison cellhouse, there are rows of cells stacked on top of one another. The cells on the second through the top floor of the cellhouse have a steel mesh walkway in front of the cells known as the walk.

X-Row The death row area of the prison. (Archaic: *C.C.'s*)

Processing

Butterfly New arrivals, who are young and pretty, at a particular prison.

Diagnostic Center *also* **Reception Center** When an inmate first arrives at a prison he is subjected to a series of psychological and intelligence tests. It is determined how dangerous he is to the public as well as to the institution. These factors are evaluated at a prison diagnostic center. These centers are normally located in a maximum security facility. The type of prison a person goes to will be based on the scores received at the diagnostic center.

Fogged De-lousing an inmate. It is customary procedure in jails and prisons to de-louse inmates as part of initial processing. When an inmate has been de-loused, he has been fogged.

Fresh Meat New inmates arriving in prison.

Merry-Go-Round Before an inmate can leave a prison he must clear all the various agencies within the institution, such as the library and recreation department. This is to insure the inmate is not in possession of any items from these agencies. The inmate is given a clearance form and signatures must be obtained from all the supervisors of each agency.

This is known as being on the merry-go-round. (Archaic: *make the rounds*)

Roll Up Any time an inmate leaves an institution, either for release, transfer to another institution, hospitalization or a court appearance. The term originated in county jails from the manner in which inmates were required to roll up their mattresses and bedding to turn in when leaving the institution.

Train Refers to prisoners being transported from one institution to another. (Archaic: *boat, draft*)

Waiting to Catch the Chain Inmates waiting to be transferred from jail to a prison. (Archaic: *ship, ride*)

Discipline

Adjustment Center Isolation or solitary confinement areas used to house inmates who are having difficulties living in general population or who are consistently in violation of prison rules.

Back on the Yard Refers to an inmate moving back into general population from isolation or protective custody. "Quig is out of the hole and back on the yard again."

Bing Solitary confinement.

Black Lock *also* **Black Lockup** An inmate in solitary confinement for disciplinary purposes is said to be behind the black lock or in the black lockup.

Box In solitary confinement for disciplinary purposes.

Checked-In *also* **Check In** When an inmate leaves the general population of the prison and enters the protective segregation unit, he is referred to as checked in. (Archaic: *get oneself a banner, get oneself sloughed up*)

Control Unit The solitary confinement area of a prison.

Crazy Alley *also* **Cranky Hatch** The segregation area of a prison reserved for the mentally unstable inmates.

Daddy Tank A segregated prison cell block reserved for lesbians or feminine homosexuals, protecting them from other inmates.

Damper *also* **Digger** The segregation unit or hole. (Archaic: *ironhouse*)

Deadlock When an inmate is on deadlock, he is locked in his cell for a certain period of time. (Archaiç: *throw the key away*)

Frog's March Frog's march is a method prison guards use to carry and transfer difficult, hard-to-handle inmates. This method consists of four officers each grabbing an arm or a leg and carrying the inmate, face down, parallel with the ground.

Ghosting *also* **Ghost Train** Ghosting is a procedure for removing prisoners from one prison and transporting them to another prison in the middle of the night. Ghosting is a necessary procedure used to break up protest movements, to hinder outside inquiries about allegations of sexual assault or beatings, to break up riots or potential riotous situations, or for prisoner safety. Ghosting takes place during the night after the entire prison has been secured to keep from arousing suspicion and causing more unrest. Ghosting is also referred to as taking the ghost train.

Going to the Bahamas Being sent to the "hole" or isolation unit.

Hole *also* **Hole Time** In prison there are rules and regulations by which inmates must live. When an inmate is found guilty of violating the more serious rules, he is sometimes placed in a segregation unit for a period of time as punishment. This segregation unit is known as the hole and the time spent there as hole time. The hole also refers to the individual isolation cells used in the segregation unit.

Even though being placed in the hole is still a dreadful experience, it is much more humane today than in the past. The hole in the past had no bed, mattress or light and had a drain hole in the center of the floor that was utilized as a toilet. A person placed in this type of hole would not see daylight for weeks at a time. (Archaic: *blue room, coop*)

Judy *also* **Jupe Balls** The name for the meals that are served in the hole or lockdown areas. This meal is part of an offender's punishment. Judy is a ground patty $4'' \times 4'' \times 3''$ that is made up of the entire meal's ingredients and is run through a grinder. They are traditionally served burned on the outside and raw on the inside.

Kangaroo Court Prison disciplinary hearings. The name implies an inmate is quickly in and out without any real justice taking place.

Klondike An individual, solitary confinement cell.

Lockdown *also* **Lockdown Time** Although prison life affords inmates a small degree of freedom within the prison, there are many periods of time when inmates are confined to their cells or housing units. These periods of time are known as lockdown or lockdown time. The frequency and length of these lockdowns varies with each institution as will the times of the day. However, lockdowns will always occur during periods of inmate head counts and throughout the night. There are also times when a person is locked down during normal release times for various administrative, investigative or disciplinary reasons. (Archaic: *limbo*)

Lockup Unit *also* **Lockup** Whenever an inmate is found guilty of violating prison rules, a customary punishment is isolation. Each prison has cellhouses or areas designated for this punishment. These areas are referred to as lockup units or lockup. (Archaic: *icebox, ironhouse, cooler, dark cell*)

On the Shelf When a prisoner is on the shelf, he is being held in solitary confinement.

P & Q P & Q stands for "Peace and Quiet" and refers to an inmate being placed in solitary confinement.

P.S. Short for protective segregation. Although P.S. literally means protective segregation, it has come to stand for "punks and snivelers." (Archaic: *isolation*)

Piss 'n' Punk Rations of bread and water which are served in the hole or lockdown situations. This practice is not widespread today. (Archaic: *angel cake & wine*)

Protective Custody A prison within a prison. Inmates are housed there for a variety of reasons ranging from the type of crime committed to their inability to live safely among the "general population." The general population look upon PC inmates with a complete distrust and feel they are "snitches" or informants for prison authorities.

PC inmates are segregated from "general population." There is no mixing between the two groups. PC units are fenced or isolated in some fashion from the other units.

Many times, during prison riots, PC areas are taken over and the inmates are subjected to extreme brutality and even death.

It should be pointed out that not all individuals who "check in" to PC units are heinous criminals or "snitches." It is common in some prisons to have men "check in" who simply need relief from the tension and hatred that runs rampant on the general yard. "Shorttimers" will also sometimes go to one of these units in an attempt to get away from any problems that might hinder their release and to avoid the wrath of other inmates who do not like the fact someone is going home. This is especially true with men who are doing long sentences. Seeing a man get parole is a constant reminder they are not going home and their anger is directed at these individuals. In most maximum security prisons, one does not boast about getting out. For safety's sake, it is something to keep to oneself.

Snitchball When inmates in the protective segregation unit of a prison are seen playing basketball or some sport, it is jokingly said they are playing snitchball.

Sol An abbreviation for solitary confinement.

Jobs

Gun Gang *also* **Chain Gang** Prisoner work details that go outside the prison to clean along the highway.

The term chain gang originated in the southern prisons where the prisoners were attached to one another with leg shackles and chains. Today, prisoners are no longer chained together but are still closely attended by armed guards, hence gun gang.

Range Tender An inmate who cleans the showers and mop room on a particular range of cells is called a range tender. Range tenders also assist inmates with daily living necessities and problems. (Archaic: *works the flats*)

Tag Shop For many years the primary industry in prison has been the making of vehicular license plates. The area where these plates are made is known as the tag shop. Although some prisons are now manufacturing many other items, license plate manufacturing is still the main industry in many prisons.

Work Gang *also* **Gang** Work crews who do the cleaning and other menial jobs around the prison grounds. These gangs are not to be confused with the gun gangs or chain gangs, although some inmates may facetiously refer to their work crew as a gun gang.

Possessions

Compliance Check All institutions have periodic room searches for "contraband." These searches are called compliance checks.

Contraband Anything not authorized by an institution. For example: tattoo equipment, metal eating utensils, alcohol and drugs. (Archaic: *stash*)

Property Anything sent to an inmate from the "outside," such as a stereo or TV. (Archaic: *relief, score, boodle*)

The Free Market

Burnt Not repaid for a loan. It is normally said in a humorous fashion between friends. "Hey Fred, when are you going to pay me back for the 'squares'?" "I'm not going to. You're burnt."

Car *also* **Cadillac** In "lockup" units or cellhouses where the prisoners are locked in their cells the majority of the time, inmates devise ingenious methods for passing cigarettes and other items from cell to cell. One of the most popular ways is to make a car or cadillac. A car is made by tearing bed sheets into long, narrow strips approximately three inches in width. These sheet strips are then tied to one another making one long strip. On one end is tied a paperback book which is actually referred to as the car. The book or car is then thrown to other cells, the item needed is tied to the book and the car is retrieved by pulling in the sheet strip. (Archaic: *trolley, passline*)

Clean It Up To explain, clarify or take care of something.

Con Job *also* **Con** Games which are run on new inmates to fool or exploit them for money or other items. (Archaic: *hook, duke in, short con*)

Cop *also* **Coppin'** To acquire something by legal or illegal means. "He copped that radio for twenty dollars."
     To cop or coppin' may be associated with feelings or emotions. "He really copped a 'buzz' from that marijuana."

Co-Sign Co-sign means to verify something. It can be qualifying a person's credit or verifying something someone has said. As some people get a bad reputation for lying or stretching the truth, they usually need several co-signers before they are believed.

Ducat A certificate stating the bearer is entitled to a certain amount of money or "store."
     Ducats are used in inmate stores since money is contraband in most prisons.

Green *also* **Green Money** Official U.S. currency. Inmates are not allowed to have money in their possession so the green money that circulates throughout the prison is contraband. Since green is illegal, it has a slightly higher value in prison and is used primarily for gambling and drug transactions. (Archaic: *spinach*)

Half Steppin' A feeble attempt at doing something. This can apply to paying debts, sports participation, prison jobs or associations with other prisoners. An inmate who serves his time half steppin' is usually not respected or trusted by other inmates.

Hustle Wages in prison are so low many inmates, in order to obtain necessities, turn to other means of making money. These other methods are called hustles. There are basically three types of hustles: natural, legal and illegal. Natural hustles are jobs that automatically place the holder in the position to earn extra money. Examples of natural hustles are: laundry workers, barbers, or kitchen workers. Some legal hustles, other than prison jobs, are shoe shining, ironing clothes, making picture frames or sewing. Some illegal hustles are selling drugs, making home brew and tattooing.

Is His Money Good? An inquiry to determine if someone is good for payment in regard to a credit transaction.

Kick Him Down *also* **Kick Me Down** When one inmate gives something to another inmate, it is known as kicking him down. When one inmate buys a "box bag" of marijuana, he may kick his friend down a "joint."

Lay a Rap To persuade. (Archaic: *duke in*)

Long An abundance of something. A person with many years to serve is said to have long time or a person with a lot of money has long money. (Archaic: *swag of*)

Mammy An abundance. A person with four cartons of cigarettes has cigarettes mammy. (Archaic: *slew of*)

My Money's Good A statement that one is good for credit.

On the Books Having money on account in your name.

Out in the Water In debt. (Archaic: *in the barrel, in the hole, on the nut*)

Slow Playin' *also* **Slow Walkin'** To stall someone. "He has been slow playin' me for three weeks and he only owes me two packs." Although there is no definite time frame, generally a person is slow walkin' if the debt goes beyond one week or the next payday.

Squash To straighten out, take care of or stop something. "I squashed that debt with my connection." (Archaic: *iron out*)

State Provisions

Issue Items similar to state issue but used on a daily and more personal basis, such as a daily issue of ice or portion of food during meals. Essentially, issue means to get your fair share. (Archaic: *state-o*)

Jumpsuits One piece, coverall jumpsuits are popular in many prisons as the official, work detail clothing. The majority of the work details assigned outside the prison use some form of jumpsuit since they are normally a bright color and easily recognized if an inmate tries to escape.

   Many prisons also utilize jumpsuits in their prisoner intake centers. Inmates are required to wear these jumpsuits while they are at the reception center until they are classified and sent to a particular prison.

State Clothes Any clothing provided by the prison. The quality of state clothes is generally so poor that most inmates try to obtain their own jeans and shirts, provided the institution allows personal clothing. State clothes seldom fit properly, they often wear poorly and are drab in color. This tends to make everyone appear the same, taking any individuality from the inmate. (Archaic: *tent*)

State Issue Anything supplied by the state for inmate use. It is primarily used to mean clothing, footwear and bedding. (Archaic: *state stuff*)

State Pay Monies earned by inmates for work performed for the state, institution or any prison job. State pay is such a small amount that it makes it difficult for an inmate to exist on this money alone. State pay ranges from fifty cents a day to approximately four dollars a day, but few inmates earn wages at the upper end of the scale.

2

SENTENCING

All Day A life sentence. "He is doing all day for murder." The amount of time an inmate with a life sentence must serve before being eligible for parole varies with each state.

All day is sometimes used to indicate an extremely long prison sentence whereby the inmate has little chance of ever being released. (Archaic: *from now on*)

Alleging Priors *also* **Sentence Enhancement** Some states have mandatory sentencing guidelines to be used for career criminals. There would be separate sentencing guidelines for the first offense, second offense, and so on, with the sentence ranges increased in each bracket. For example: Using a Class 2 felony in the first offense sentencing bracket, the sentence may be 7 to 21 years in prison. A Class 2 felony conviction in the second offense bracket may be 14 to 28 years in prison. And a Class 2 felony conviction in the third offender bracket may be 21 to 35 years in prison. This is commonly known as sentence enhancement or alleging priors.

Back Time *also* **Jail Time** Time spent in jail while awaiting trial and sentencing. This time is credited against the amount of time of your sentence. Thus, if you spend six months in jail and get an 18-month sentence, you will have six months back time and will now have to serve 12 months. (Archaic: *jawbone time*)

Bad Rap A long prison sentence, usually more than 20 years.

Bank *also* **Make** To prove someone guilty of committing a crime. Banking someone generally results in that person's going to prison.

Beef A beef is a crime or charge of a crime. "He received a beef for having that stolen radio in his cell."

Bit A prison sentence or the amount of time a person has to spend in prison. "He has a twenty-five-year bit for murder."
Bit is occasionally used to indicate a person's charges or crime—as in "He was charged with another bit." (Archaic: *jolt*)

B.O.T. When an inmate is placed on parole, he has a certain amount of prison time still remaining that the state allows him to serve on parole. If an inmate violates his parole and is sent back to prison, the "balance of time" he has left to serve in prison is referred to as his "B.O.T."

Bowlegged Multiple prison sentences that are to be served consecutively.

Bum Rap When a person is falsely accused or convicted of a crime, it is said he was given a bum rap. "He really didn't do anything. The burglary charge is a bum rap." (Archaic: *bum finger*)

Buried An inmate with a life sentence. Buried may also be used to indicate a long prison sentence, usually 20 years or more.

Butt The final portion of an inmate's prison sentence. The length of time of a "butt" depends upon the length of the original sentence. A person with a two-year sentence may refer to the last three to six months as the "butt" of his sentence, whereas an inmate with a 20-year sentence, or more, may refer to the final two years as the butt of his sentence. Generally, the final year of a prison sentence is known as the butt. Butt only refers to time spent in prison, not parole time.

Case An inmate's charge or crime for which he was convicted and sentenced is his case. Case may be used to indicate the entire set of circumstances used against someone or just the charge for which he was convicted and sentenced.

The term case may be used for charges received while in prison, either for new "street" charges or for offenses committed in prison. "He 'copped' a new case for dealing drugs."

Commute *also* **Commutation of Sentence** A type of pardon by the governor or board of paroles and pardons which can have numerous conditions attached to it. It should be noted some states now have sentencing statutes which make it impossible for a commutation of a sentence until a specific amount of time is served. (Archaic: *chop a bit*)

Concurrent Sentence When an individual is sentenced to two or more prison sentences concurrently, he can serve them all at the same time. For example: If an individual is sentenced to three five-year prison sentences to be served concurrently, he can serve all three sentences at once, thereby serving only five years in prison.

Consecutive Sentence When an individual is sentenced to two or more sentences consecutively, the first sentence must be served in its entirety before the second one can be served.

Deuce A two-year prison sentence. (Archaic: *two spaces, two-spotter*)

Deuce and a Quarter A 2- to 25-year prison sentence.

Dime A 10-year prison sentence. (Archaic: *sawbuck, sawski*)

Discount Justice The practice of allowing alleged criminals to plead guilty to a lesser offense than the one originally charged to receive a lesser sentence. This enables the state to save the expense that a trial by jury would incur, but also gives the state a conviction in that case. It also usually enables the criminal to receive a shorter prison sentence thereby making discount justice attractive for both the prosecution and the defense.

Doing the Book A life sentence. Can also mean a person was sentenced to the full extent of the law. (Archaic: *bookful*)

Dumptruck An attorney, usually a public defender. Because of the huge caseloads and the high number of plea agreements, inmates feel they are being sentenced by the truck load. (Archaic: *tongue, warbler*)

Fall *also* **Take a Fall** *and* **Fall Guy** A prison sentence. "Jim fell for ten years for bank robbery."

Taking a fall is to be arrested, convicted and sentenced to serve time in prison. When two or more people are arrested for the same crime, one of the defendants may take the fall for the others by confessing he committed the crime alone, so that he is the only one to go to prison.

The terms take a fall and fall guy originated in 1922 when Albert Bacon Fall, then secretary of the interior of the United States, accepted full responsibility in the Teapot Dome scandal. He and a number of his colleagues were investigated for leasing land in the Teapot Dome Reserve, in Wyoming, to private oil interests. To save his friends, Albert Fall took the entire blame and served one year and a day in federal prison. (Archaic: *take the knock*)

Flat Bit A prison sentence that is fully served with no time off for good behavior.

Habitual Criminal Sentence Allows the state to impose an extra sentence to criminals with three or more unrelated felony convictions. These sentences may range from 5 to 25 years, and this sentence must be served consecutive to any other sentence the individual receives. The amount of time by which a sentence is enhanced will vary from state to state, but it is usually 1 to 30 years or a life sentence. (Archaic: *The Bitch*)

Indeterminate Sentencing An indeterminate sentence is a sentence range imposed to a convicted felon requiring the inmate to serve no less than a minimum number and no more than a maximum number of years, for example: A person convicted of a particular crime may be sentenced to a prison term of no less than two years and no more than ten years. This is called a two- to ten-year sentence. The inmate would have to serve two years before being considered for release, but he could not be forced to serve more than ten years. Under this type of sentence, it would be the responsibility of the parole board to determine when the individual should be released. (Archaic: *garter*)

Jacked Up When a person is charged with a crime, it is known as being jacked up. Jacked up may refer to anyone being charged with a crime, but it is used more often to indicate an inmate being charged with a new crime while in prison.

Long Bit A long prison sentence, usually longer than ten years.

Mandatory Sentencing A strict sentencing guide for each class of felony crime. All states classify their felony crimes by either an A, B, C method or a 1, 2, 3 method, with A or 1 being the most severe and E or 5 being the least severe. For each class felony there will be a minimum and a maximum amount of time which can be imposed. For example: a Class 2 or Class B felony conviction may call for a sentence in the range between 7 and 21 years. The sentencing judge is bound to this sentence range and must impose a sentence somewhere in this 7- to 21-year range bracket.

Under mandatory sentencing, the judge cannot impose a lesser sentence than what the sentence guidelines require. Because of this, some states have now altered their sentence guidelines to allow the sentencing judge to impose a more lenient sentence if he feels the circumstances warrant it. This allows the sentencing judge to impose probation, a suspended sentence or some other type of sentence that would let the defendant bear his punishment without going to prison. This could be a drug rehabilitation program or community service. These more lenient sentences are usually only given to first-time, non-dangerous offenders.

Mouthpiece An attorney. (Archaic: *cop a plea, two-bit mouthpiece*)

Natural Life An inmate with a natural life sentence will have to spend his entire life in prison without hope of being granted parole. (Archaic: *the rosary*)

Nickel A five-year prison sentence. In prison, the number of years of sentences are often referred to as monetary coin amounts. (Archaic: *fin, handful, pound*)

O.R. *also* **Own Recognizance** To be released from jail after being formally charged with a crime. This is done under the condition the individual will make all court appearances. (Archaic: *D.O.R. — discharged on your own recognizance*)

Play Play is used when someone is requesting leniency in court or in prison for a violation of prison rules — as in: "I hope I get some play tomorrow in court."

Plea Agreement *also* **Plea Bargain** Many times the prosecuting attorney and the defendant will enter a plea agreement, commonly called a plea bargain. A plea agreement is when the prosecuting attorney and the defendant agree on a specified sentence for a particular crime in exchange for a guilty plea from the defendant. In a plea agreement, all terms of the sentence are specified, such as prison time, fine, restitution and special conditions, such as community service. There are two basic types of plea agreements: fixed plea agreement and open end plea agreement.

A fixed plea agreement is one in which the prosecutor and defendant agree to an exact specified sentence. For example: A defendant accused of committing a Class 2 felony may be facing a prison sentence of 7 to 21 years. If he and the prosecutor agree that a 10-year prison sentence is fair, they will enter a plea agreement with the 10-year sentence guaranteed in exchange for a guilty plea. Both the prosecutor and defendant would then sign the plea agreement and the sentencing judge would impose the sentence.

An open end plea agreement is one in which the defendant agrees to plea guilty to a felony charge without having the sentence specified. It would then be up to the sentencing judge to determine what sentence to impose according to the state's sentencing guidelines. For example: A defendant may agree to plead guilty to a Class 2 felony with a sentencing range of 7 to 21 years in prison. By signing an open end plea agreement, he would be putting his fate in the hands of the sentencing judge by allowing him to impose a prison sentence somewhere in the 7- to 21-year range. The judge would review all the circumstances of the crime and impose whatever sentence he felt the crime necessitated.

Plea agreements are generally advantageous to both

parties. For the defendant, it is usually a lesser sentence than he would receive if he went through trial and was convicted. It also spares him the embarrassment of a public trial. For the prosecutor, it saves time and taxpayer money because the case does not go to trial.

In the term plea bargain, the word "bargain," comes from the manner in which the agreement is negotiated. There will usually be some dickering, or bargaining, before a compromise is reached. (Archaic: *cop out*)

Quarter A 25-year prison sentence. (Archaic: *twenty-five boffos*)

Rap The crime a person committed or the crime he is charged with committing. "He just got another burglary rap." (Archaic: *knock*)

Another usage for rap is in reference to a person's particular area of expertise in crime — "His rap is embezzlement."

Ride the Beef Taking the blame for a disciplinary infraction in prison or for a criminal charge. "Get that 'weed' out of here. I'm not going to ride the beef for your stupidity."

Running Together *also* **Concurrent Sentence** When a person receives multiple prison sentences to be served concurrently, the sentences are referred to as running together.

Concurrent prison sentences signify the inmate serves the sentences at the same time with the longest sentence taking precedent as to parole and release dates.

Running Wild *also* **Stacked** *or* **Consecutive Sentence** When a person receives multiple prison sentences that must be served consecutively.

Consecutive prison sentences signify the inmate must complete one sentence before serving the next one. (Archaic: *life on the installment plan*)

Street Beef Inmates sometimes commit crimes that warrant new "street" charges requiring trial procedures in the state court system. These new charges are referred to as street beefs. An inmate may be street beefed for various crimes, some of which are murder, drug possession, sexual assault and escape.

Stretch Time spent in prison. "Phil is doing another stretch for burglary." (Archaic: *piece, ride, trick*)

Suspended Sentence A prison sentence which grants probation in lieu of going to prison. If the person successfully completes the probation, the prison sentence will be expired. If the individual violates the probation, he would then be sent to prison to serve the sentence. (Archaic: *draw, an s.s.*)

Turned State When a person testifies in court for the prosecution against a friend or "crime partner," it is referred to as turning state. A person who turned state informed on someone for some illegal activity. This is usually done with a promise of leniency from the prosecuting attorney. Most people who have turned state go directly to a protective segregation unit when they enter prison. (Archaic: *turn copper*)

Twenty-Five to Life *also* **Quarter to Life** *and* **All Day from a Quarter** A prison sentence that requires the inmate to serve no less than 25 years, up to life. (Archaic: *phony-baloney life*)

Two to Ten A two- to ten-year prison sentence whereby the inmate must serve no less than two years and no more than ten years. (Archaic: *split bit*)

Walk To be found not guilty of criminal charges. An inmate who has criminal charges dismissed or is released of all obligations concerning something illegal can also walk. "I'll walk on the armed robbery charge, but they'll convict me for stealing."

Wino Time A short sentence. "I wish he would quit complaining. He isn't doing nothin' but wino time." (Archaic: *sleeping time*)

Yard A 100-year prison sentence. (Archaic: *one hundred smackers*)

3

SERVING TIME

Ain't Got But a Minute An expression used in reference to someone who is getting close to his release date. (Archaic: *coming down the hill*)

Behind the Iron Door In prison.

Boomerang Coming back to prison immediately after being released. (Archaic: *coming back for seconds*)

Chronophobic A person who has a fear of doing time in prison.

Copper Time In many prisons there is a form of copper time which is time off for good behavior. "With copper time I am getting one day off for every two I serve."

Dead Time Used to describe the manner in which some inmates in general population serve their prison sentence. Even though they have access to programs and activities, they do not take advantage of these privileges.

Do Bird To serve time in prison.

Do Your Own Time Mind your own business and do not get involved in all the "cons" or "games" that are constantly being played. Many men come to prison unaware of what to expect and end up getting involved in other people's business or "games." This will ultimately lead them into a great deal of trouble.

Doing the Book An inmate serving a life sentence.

Doing Time A common term indicating a person is in prison. (Archaic: *doing penance*)

Down A person is down when he is in prison. "Fred has been down for ten years." Down refers to a person being in prison, not the prison sentence itself. (Archaic: *stored away, up the river*)

Dressed In When a person first arrives in prison he is issued prison clothing. This clothing is new, usually oversized and easily recognizable by the other inmates. The conspicuous new inmate is referred to as dressed in.

Dropped in the Bucket Placed in prison.

Easy Time An inmate who serves his time with few troubles or hardships. This is usually accomplished by staying busy and making efforts to better oneself. (Archaic: *light time*)

Fish *also* **Fish Number** An inmate new to a particular corrections system in any given state. Since most states have several prisons, an inmate new to a certain prison would not necessarily be a fish. An inmate is considered to be a fish only when he is new to the system and is generally considered a fish for three to six months.

Every state has a numbering system for all the inmates in its prison system. Each prisoner is assigned a Department of Corrections (D.O.C.) number and these numbers increase in conjunction with the number of inmates received. Therefore, a prisoner with a new or high number within that system is said to have a fish number. A fish is easily detected by the high number he is assigned. (Archaic: *new fish*)

Flat Time A defendant sentenced to flat time must serve every day of the imposed sentence before being released. (Archaic: *flat bit*)

Good Time Time an inmate can earn for good behavior. This good time will apply towards the amount of time an inmate must serve before being released. Generally, the amount of good time a person can earn is predetermined by his specific sentencing structure. Some sentences require an inmate to serve two or more days in prison before he can earn one day of good time. Some sentences allow an inmate to earn one day of good time for every day served in prison. Other, more lenient sentences allow an inmate to earn two or even three days for every day served.

In addition to the good time that is predetermined by specific sentences, many states offer other ways to earn good time. Some states have fire-fighting crews who can earn from one to seven days of good time for each day they spend fighting fires. Some states reward their fire-fighting crews by granting from one to four months of extra good time for each year they serve on the fire-fighting crew.

Many states are now awarding extra good time to inmates who earn their high school general equivalency degree (GED) or other educational achievement. Some states offer good time for giving blood. Some states even offer good time for minimum security inmates who work in community service related jobs, such as maintenance work for the elderly.

With all the various ways inmates may earn good time, it would appear that a person could serve a prison sentence in a relatively short period of time. It should be noted that this most always is not true. Judges and prosecuting attorneys are well aware of their state's good time structure and take this into consideration before imposing prison sentences. For example: Under the half-time structure, if a judge determines that a person should serve five years in prison for a specific crime, he might sentence that individual to ten years, or more.

Hard Time An inmate who has difficulty serving his prison sentence. Hard time may be caused by disciplinary problems, family problems, money problems, etc. Some inmates never adapt to prison life and serve their entire sentence as hard time.

Hard time also refers to a sentencing procedure whereby the defendant is required to serve two-thirds of the imposed sentence before being eligible for parole. (Archaic: *do tough time, bring time the hard way*)

Hell's Front Porch *also* **Devil's Front Porch** In prison.

Hit the Pit To be jailed or imprisoned.

Hole Time Time spent in isolation. Since time spent in the "hole" does not ordinarily allow the inmate to accumulate any "good time," it is referred to as dead time. Hole time is also called dead time due to the fact that inmates do not have access to any educational or recreational programs since they are locked in their cell at all times. (Archaic: *box time*)

I'm Too Short to Get in a Conversation with You. I Might Have to Leave in the Middle of It! A familiar, humorous expression made in jest by someone close to his release date.

Jump Street The very start or beginning of something. "I told him from jump street I couldn't pay him till next week." (Archaic: *pop off*)

Kiss the Baby A guaranteed prison sentence. "He robbed the bank, now he can kiss the baby."

Life on the Installment Plan Coming back to prison repeatedly. "Hey Hank, back again? What are you doing, life on the installment plan?"

Lockdown Time *also* **Count Time** The time an inmate spends in his cell. Inmates are "locked down" for various reasons, the most common being during head count. Inmates are also "locked down" throughout the night. "Lockdown time begins at 9 P.M. and ends at 5 A.M."

Long *also* **Longtimer** An inmate with many years to serve. Although a prison sentence of 10 years or more is generally considered to be long, it is more frequently associated with prison sentences of 25 years to life. (Archaic: *bundle, chunk, package*)

On Ice In prison. (Archaic: *inside*)

Out to Pasture *also* **Big Pasture** Being in prison.

Short *also* **Shorttimer** An inmate with only a few years to serve. Although a prison sentence of less than ten years is generally considered short, it is more frequently associated with prison sentences of one to five years.
Short may be used to indicate a person has served the

majority of his sentence and is near his release date. A person who has served 12 years of a 15-year sentence is now short.

Even though a two- or three-year prison sentence may sound short, in reality there is no short time. When you are actually serving a two-year sentence one day at a time, it does not seem short at all. (Archaic: *over the hump*)

Soft Time A sentencing system under which an inmate must serve one-half the imposed sentence before being eligible for parole. This does not mean the inmate will automatically be granted parole since there are other requirements and obligations that must be met. (Archaic: *soft bit*)

Standin' on Your Head When a person is sentenced to a small amount of time he feels he can serve with relative ease, it is said he can do that time standin' on his head.

An inmate who has served the majority of a prison sentence and is getting close to the release date is referred to as being able to finish his sentence standin' on his head. (Archaic: *on one ear*)

State Raised Originally, an inmate who had been in and out of prison all his life, serving the majority of his teen years and young adulthood in institutions. The definition has since expanded to include any inmate who relies solely on the prison for existence. These inmates have no family or friends who can help support them while incarcerated.

An inmate who never misses a prison meal or is always wearing new state-issue prison clothing is referred to as state raised in jest by his friends. (Archaic: *found a home*)

Stir Crazy Some men who come to prison cannot mentally adjust to the many hours of continuous confinement in their cells. These inmates suffer from extreme anxiety and are referred to as being stir crazy. (Archaic: *stir-bug, dingaling*)

Time Class *also* **Parole Class** A disciplinary structure which sets the guidelines for "good time." In order for an inmate to receive the maximum amount of "good time" his particular sentence allows, he must be in Time Class I. For example: A state in the midwest has a half-time sentencing structure where an inmate is granted one day of "good time" for each day he serves in prison. Therefore, if an inmate remains in Time Class I the entire time he is in prison, he will be released when he serves one-half of the imposed sentence. Each state has different amounts of "good time" granted for each time class, but a general guideline is: Time Class I means an inmate is earning the maximum amount of "good time" his particular sentence allows. Time Class II means an inmate is earning one-half of the maximum allowable amount of "good time." Time Class III means an inmate is not earning any "good time" at all. Some states have their time class structure divided into four classes. In that type of system, Time Class IV would be the time class that grants no good time.

Wake Up An inmate's last morning in prison. "I got three days and a wake up before I go home." (Archaic: *flop, roll-over*)

Whale Number *also* **Whalie** As each inmate enters a prison system, he is assigned a D.O.C. number. A person who has a D.O.C. number 10,000 greater than another inmate is said to have his whale number. An inmate who has a D.O.C. number 10,000 greater than another is sometimes referred to as his whalie.

Years ago, a whale number was normally 1,000 greater than another inmate's number. For example: D.O.C. #4858 is the whale number for an inmate with #3858. This was probably due to the fact that not nearly as many people were being sentenced to prison and thus it took longer for a thousand inmates to be sentenced. (Archaic: *relief, one's fish*)

4

INMATES

Characteristics

Break Weak An expression to indicate a person's behavior when they back down or become passive in a confrontative situation. "There's no need to ask Dave to join us, he'll only break weak."

Buff Up *also* **Buffed** To add muscle mass to one's body by rigorous weightlifting exercises.
A buffed inmate is one who has large muscles as a direct result of weightlifting.

Can't Hang An inmate who cannot survive in the general population of a prison and must "check in" to the "PC" unit.

Chilly Describes a person who is lacking in emotion, compassion or friendliness. Insults or rude remarks said to or about someone are called chilly.
It may also be used as a compliment to one's ability or skill, but this is rare.

Cold Blooded *also* **Cold** Although cold or cold blooded are sometimes used to mean unemotional and compassionless, in prison jargon it is more frequently used as a compliment of one's skill or ability. "That Bill is a cold blooded basketball player."
Cold may also be used to describe someone who is good at what he does.

Con Wise When a person has been incarcerated for several years, he learns the nuances of prison life: how to get things accomplished, get a good job, etc. Once he acquires this knowledge, he is said to be con wise. Con wise is defined differently by prison administrators. To them, a person who is con wise is one who manipulates the system to his own advantage. (Archaic: *joint wise, stir wise*)

Done an About Face A person has changed. The change can be from good to bad or bad to good.

Flag *also* **Flyin' a Flag** A label (usually negative) placed on someone for a particular characteristic he may possess. "He was flagged a homosexual before anyone really knew him."
   A person is flyin' a flag when he is allowing other inmates to see his particular character traits in his appearance or actions. "He is flying his homosexual flag."

Front Street Front street is an expression used when something is made known to other people or they are allowed to become aware of certain things. "You put me on front street when you told him I took his radio."
   Front street may be used when business dealings or private lives are made known to everyone, as when a drug dealer lets it be known he is dealing drugs. "He put his business on front street."

Hangin' on the Leg *also* **Leg Hanger** To fraternize eagerly with prison staff. Hangin' on the leg, in prison, is a disgusting form of fraternization as it is a general rule of inmates not to associate with prison guards or staff members. Prison staff have no respect for leg hangers.

Heart Courage. Heart is an important and valuable characteristic to have in prison as the stronger inmates or "vultures" will prey on the weaker prisoners. An inmate may not have the actual physical size or ability to defend himself, but he must have the heart to prove he will retaliate in some way. (Archaic: *balls, clock, movie, ticker*)

Hip *also* **Hep** A person who is knowledgeable in a particular subject or aware of all the complexities of a particular subject. When an inmate is knowledgeable and aware of the many aspects of prison life, he is referred to as being hip to prison. (Archaic: *slick*)

Keeping a Low Profile Staying out of the way of guards and other staff members. These people are not looking for trouble.

Know What Time It Is Know all the facts of a particular situation. An inmate may suspect his wife is having an affair. Since he is not absolutely sure, he only thinks he knows what time it is with her. He does not actually know what time it is until he learns all the facts of the situation.

Laying Track Lying to other inmates. "You never know when to believe Dave. He is always laying track."
  Also used in reference to someone who sets a precedent in a certain situation.

Out of the Pocket A person who acts abnormally or contrary to his usual behavior. "Harold is out of the pocket."

Pull His Covers *also* **Pulling Covers** When someone's true identity or characteristics are revealed. "He pulled Bob's covers when he told everyone that Bob is a snitch."

Pull Someone's Coat To bring something to one's attention or make him aware of certain things. "He pulled my coat when he told me Rick is a snitch."

Putting Your Business on the Street Making certain things about yourself known to other inmates.

Rah Rah A female inmate who eagerly fraternizes with guards and prison officials.

Scandalous A compliment of one's skill or ability. An inmate who is extremely adept at something is said to be scandalous.

Shopping Looking for something to steal.

Slick A criminal's specialty or field of expertise. "Jim's slick is bank robbery."

Slick Leg When person is innocent of any wrongdoing. "Ted is slick leg."
Also may indicate that a person was too smart to get caught, even though he may have done something illegal.

Solid Con *also* **Stand-Up Convict** A trustworthy and well-respected inmate. The prison code of ethics places a solid con near the top of the prison population.

Stick *also* **Sharp Stick** *and* **Long Stick** A person's influence or clout. When a person has a great deal of influence and can get things accomplished, he is said to have a sharp stick. An abundance of stick is referred to as long stick.

Stone Taking something to the extreme. "Tom is stone crazy," meaning Tom is completely crazy or "Chuck is a stone junkie," meaning he is a serious heroin addict.

Under Cover Trying to keep something a secret. An under cover homosexual is a man trying to keep this fact a secret from the majority of the prison population.

Wearing Your Business An expression used to mean a person is visually allowing his affairs to be known to other inmates. "That homosexual is wearing his business, he must be on the make."

Types

Accelerator A person imprisoned for committing arson.
May also be used to indicate the flammable substance arsonists use to start fires.

Asocial *also* **A-Soc'** A person in prison for committing sex crimes.

Auxiliary Cop *also* **State Con** An inmate who conducts himself in such a manner to appear more like an employee of the prison than a prisoner. These inmates may hold jobs of minor authority over other prisoners, be in charge of certain supplies or fraternize with guards. State cons rarely associate with other inmates. (Archaic: *badge man*)

Bible Thumper An inmate who becomes consumed by religion during incarceration. This may be genuine or merely a way to cope with prison life. (Archaic: *Jesus stiff, psalm-singing muzzler*)

Canary *also* **Nightingale** A police informant and or a prison snitch.

Cheese Eater *also* **Cheese Pride** *and* **Cheesey Rider** Expressions used sarcastically in reference to a "snitch" or "rat."

Chester the Molester An inmate who is in prison for sexual deviancy, whether it is rape or child molestation.

Cho-mo An inmate who is in prison for child molestation.

Chump A derogatory term for a male inmate meaning he is homosexual and or weak. To call a person a chump will usually result in a fight if the person is willing to protect his reputation. (Archaic: *lob*)

Cops Short for convicts on patrol. A female inmate who tells prison authorities of illegal activities on the "yard."

Cunt Used to refer to another woman in a most derogatory and contemptible manner.

Diddler *also* **Short Eyes** An inmate who is in prison for child molestation.

Duck An insulting term meaning gullible fool. It is usually used in a good-natured and humorous way. "Hey Joey, you really believed me when I told you they were giving us all a weekend pass. What a duck you are!" (Archaic: *dingaling*)

Featherwood Can be used as a derogatory or friendly term for a white female inmate depending on how it is used.

Highbinder A criminal or prison inmate.

Jerkwater One who is slow witted. (Archaic: *pop corn*)

Joint Man An inmate who conducts himself in such a manner that resembles a guard or employee, rather than a prisoner.

Lame *also* **Duck** Similar to a lop, only to a lesser degree. (Archaic: *as'ole*)

Lop *also* **Lop Head** A stupid and ignorant individual.
The word originated from the phrase "loss of privileges." This is a form of punishment for inmates whereby they cannot use the store or have access to other inmate privileges. (Archaic: *jerk*)

Noser A prison informant.

Pamper Pirate An inmate who is in prison for child molestation.

Pamper Sniffer An inmate who is in prison for child molestation.

Riding the Broom Conveying threats or intimidation to other women prisoners.
A woman is also riding the broom when she prophesies something may or will happen to someone.

Short Eyes A person in prison who has committed child molestation or other related crimes.

Snitch *also* **Rat** An informant.
To snitch is to tell prison authorities of illegal activities. The prison code of ethics places a snitch at the lowest level of the prison population, and if discovered, he faces physical harm and even death. For this reason, most snitches must enter protective segregation for their safety. (Archaic: *crimp, shit-heel, buzz man, belcher*)

Square Anyone not knowledgeable in a certain subject or area of life. (Archaic: *up and up ghee*)

Square John *also* **Square Johnnin'** A person who leads a legal life.
May also be a person ignorant of a certain lifestyle or subject. (Archaic: *square plug*)

Stool Pigeon *also* **Stoolie** An old term for informant. (Archaic: *stool, stoolo*)

Straight John *also* **Straight Johnnin'** An ex-convict, recently released from prison, who is now leading a legal existence. This individual is a straight john and his new lifestyle is straight johnnin'. Although there is an expression given to a recent, successful parolee, it may be used in reference to someone in prison who has changed his lifestyle and is now going straight. (Archaic: *chump, scissor-bill, dinner pailer*)

Tree Jumper *also* **Skinner** *and* **Rape-O** An inmate who is in prison for rape. (Archaic: *short arm heister, short arm bandit*)

Walkie-Talkie An inmate who is frequently seen talking to guards or staff. This type of behavior makes other convicts highly suspicious.

Willie Lump Lump *also* **Willie Lunch Meat** An idiot. (Archaic: *apsay*)

Yardbird Lawyer *also* **Jailhouse Lawyer** An inmate who develops a loathing for the criminal justice system because of its inconsistencies and perceived unfairness, and spends much of his time studying the law. Prison administrators have a dislike for such inmates and view them as troublemakers. (Archaic: *hapas capas, writ bug*)

Zuch An informant.

5

ASSOCIATES

Family & Friends

Ace-Deuce *also* **Acey-Deucey** Old prison expressions used to signify best friends.

Bunkie A light-hearted reference to a cell mate.

Cellie *also* **Cell Mate** *and* **Cell Partner** Someone who shares a cell with another person. Although cellies generally grow to be friends, they do not necessarily begin that way as most of the double bunking decisions are controlled by the institution.

Home Boy *also* **Homie** *and* **Homes** Someone from the same city, county or state as another person. In larger cities, home boys may be restricted to certain neighborhoods, whereas, in other situations, a person's home boy may be from the same city, state or geographic region.

Home Slice *also* **Home Dirt** Someone from the same city, state or geographic region as another person.

In the Car *also* **Out of the Car** When a person is a friend of someone. Conversely, when he no longer is a friend of that person, group or clique, he is said to be out of the car.

Kick It To associate or hang out together. "Let's go out on the yard and kick it for a while."

Lonely Hearts Lonely men who correspond with women in prison. In contrast to "sponsors," lonely hearts rarely send money or gifts.

Look Out for Someone Doing a favor for someone, repaying a favor or repaying a loan with interest. When an inmate is locked up in segregation for disciplinary or investigative reasons, his friends will often send him cigarettes, personal hygiene necessities and other items to which he has no access. This is referred to as looking out for him. This inmate, when released from isolation, would then look out for his benefactors by giving them a little extra, to show his appreciation, when repaying the items he received. Looking out for someone is not limited to prisoners in lockup units. An inmate may look out for his barber or laundry man by giving him something extra when paying for these services, provided he has done a good job. An inmate may request a favor from someone by telling him he will look out for him the next time he goes to the store. This implies he will buy something for him if he does the favor. It is a routine practice in prison to look out for someone who does something for you.

Outs When a person is no longer friends with someone or they no longer share certain things. Outs is also used to indicate a person is no longer welcome in a clique or gang.

Pahtner A close friend. A pahtner may also be a business associate or a workmate. (Archaic: *sidekick*)

People The family or close friends of an inmate. "My people are going to hire a new attorney for me."

Raw Jaw To ignore or refuse to speak to someone. "The teacher raw jaws me because he thinks I ask too many questions."

Roadie *also* **Road Dog** A good friend. This is someone with whom a person has a close association. The terms roadie and road dog are derived from the fact that these individuals are always seen with one another. (Archaic: *yuk*)

Roomie Someone who shares a living space with another inmate.

Running Partner A seldom used term that means a good friend.

Shine a Person On *also* **Put Him on Shine** To completely disassociate from or ignore someone.

Sponsors *also* **Financiers** Men who send money and other items to women in prison.

Trick A name women use in reference to men who are willing and eager to send them money or gifts. Inmates who are easily exploited for money and gifts are also known as tricks.

Your Chin Is Scraped from Falling Out of the Car A humorous expression said in a teasing manner to indicate a person will no longer be included in his friend's activities. This is always said in jest.

Criminal Associates

Button A lookout. An inmate keeping watch for prison guards or officials while an illegal activity is taking place. To button is to be a lookout. "Do you want me to button for you while you are doing that tattoo?" (Archaic: *gapper, hawk, jigger*)

Crime Partner *also* **Fall Partner** When two or more people are involved in the same crime, convicted and sentenced to prison for that crime. Refers only to individuals who commit crimes together. (Archaic: *ghee one hustles with*)

Drop a Dime To tell prison authorities of illegal activities someone has committed.

Give Him Up *also* **Give You Up** To turn someone in to the police or prison authorities for an illegal act he has committed. Give him up is generally associated with "crime partners." (Archaic: *dog it, cross up*)

Pin A female keeping watch for prison guards or officials while an illegal activity is taking place. Pin is also used as a verb. "Will you pin for us while we smoke this joint?"

Point *also* **Keep Point** *and* **On Point** A lookout for prison guards or officials while an illegal activity is being performed.

Rappie When two or more people are involved in the same crime, convicted and sentenced to prison for that crime. Contrary to "crime partner," rappie may be used in reference to individuals who are in prison on the same type felony conviction but unrelated cases. (Archaic: *partner on the rap*)

Roll Over To turn someone in to prison authorities for an illegal act he has committed. This is ordinarily done amongst people who have committed crimes together. (Archaic: *belch*)

Sing Like a Bird *also* **Bird Seed** An inmate informant who tells prison authorities of illegal activities is referred to as singin' like a bird.

Gangs

AB Stands for Aryan Brotherhood and is a white supremacist gang found primarily in the prisons of the southwest and west coast.

Affiliated Being close friends with or having business dealings with a gang.

American Nazi There are many gangs under the umbrella of the American Nazi gang. The common denominator is a philosophy of white supremacy. These groups are popular in the northwestern United States.

Blood In, Blood Out An expression which means only those who take a life can be a member of a particular gang and the only way to leave the gang is to be killed.

Button-Hole When gangs recruit new members, the interview and test of the prospective member is normally conducted in private. In order to get the potential member to a private meeting with gang officers, he must be slipped away from the routine prison activities to a secret rendezvous. This act of eluding is known as button-holing. To slip away is to button-hole. A variation of button-holing is when inmates slip away from work details. "He button-holed the rake crew again."

Earn Your Colors To have become a full-fledged member of a gang and have the right to get the gang's tattoo.

El Rukns Gangs found in the midwest and eastern regions of the United States.

Field Marshal A gang officer who coordinates fights or gang activities.

Field marshals are occasionally used to recruit new members.

Gangster When one of the meaner, stronger inmates uses force and intimidation to achieve things, he is referred to as a gangster.

To gangster something is to take it by force.

Get Your Bones To get your gang's tattoo.

Holder Much of the drug traffic in prison is controlled by the various gangs. This is well known and, consequently, gang members are always under suspicion and frequently searched. Therefore, it is important for gangs to have someone, who is not directly associated with them and is not a drug user, to keep drugs for them until they are sold. Such a person is referred to as a holder.

Independent An inmate who is not affiliated with a gang. While this may apply to any ethnic group, it is usually used in reference to a white person.

Mau Maus Black gangs found throughout the United States prison system.

Mexican Mafia A network of Mexican gangs found throughout the western and southwestern United States.

On My Skin In prison, gangs are primarily composed of a certain race, whether it is white, black or brown. Racial tension and separation are facts of life and within each gang there is a code of honor. When one gang member tells another something, he may be asked if he is telling the truth. His reply of verification would be — on my skin. This is the most significant word of honor a person can give, whether he is black, brown or white. On my skin is simply a way of assuring someone something is true. It is never used in jest.

Outfit Used to indicate Italian mafia gangs found throughout the United States.

Patch A gang insignia.

Political Gang membership in prison is taken very seriously. It is not simply being a member of a particular gang, it is a way of life. Gang members believe, beyond a shadow of a doubt, in gang unity, and the welfare of the gang always comes first. This way of thinking and living is referred to as political. Gang members live and die according to this political lifestyle.

Political Tats Tattoos that represent gang insignia or membership.
   Many inmates who are not gang members get political tats. In certain instances gang members will make these individuals remove their tattoos, especially if their behavior is in opposition to the gang's philosophy.
   Some gang members are called gangsters.

Probate A person who is trying to become a member of a gang. While he is on this probational status, he must do everything he is told by full-fledged members.

Rags *also* **Colors** Any clothing, bandanas, patches or insignias worn by gang members to indicate gang membership.

Rounder A mafia type gang member. Rounder is also used to mean any gangster type person.

Satellites Individuals who associate with gang members but are not members themselves.

Soldier *also* **Warrior** A gang member. Most gangs have certain members designated as soldiers who do most of the fighting and killing while the gang leaders stay removed from the violence.

Tip A gang.

War Lord One of the leaders of a gang who leads other members into gang fights and killings. A war lord is higher in rank than a soldier but is not necessarily'number one in command.

6

COMMUNICATION

Expressions

All Right A greeting used when seeing a friend or acquaintance, replacing "hi" or "hello."
    All right can also be a response to any salutary greeting to signify everything is fine or as well as can be expected. (Archaic: *howzit, what's hot*)

Bogus Not genuine. Of poor quality. Not true. Not legitimate. (Archaic: *eighteen carat*)

Bunk Bad or not good. Usually used in describing the quality of a given drug in a business transaction. "That dope that Bob has is pure bunk." (Archaic: *bum*)

Clean It Up Then Details of incidents or conversations often become distorted as they are passed from one inmate to another. When an inmate attempts to clarify these facts, he may be jeered by his friends to clean it up then. "Hey fellas, I didn't mean it that way." "Clean it up then, punk, or we will kick your ass." Although the phrase is used in fun among friends, it is sometimes used in a threatening manner in serious situations.

Didn't I? *also* **Wouldn't I?** These are expressions used emphatically in response to certain questions or statements. Didn't I? means you did and Wouldn't I? means you would. For example, a person may ask you — "Did you win that bet? and you

45

would reply—Didn't I? meaning you did, or "Would you marry her?" and you reply—Wouldn't I? meaning you would. These expressions are another way of saying yes.

Don't Try It An expression used by inmates to show they do not believe what someone is telling them. This may be used in reference to an exaggeration or an absolute lie.

How Can I Tell? Used to question the validity of a statement—"I can bench press 450 lbs." Another inmate would reply, "How can I tell?" thus questioning the statement daring the first inmate to prove it. May also be used by friends in jest in a teasing manner. "I have plenty of coffee." The reply might be, "How can I tell?" In other words, "Since I haven't been offered any, how do I know you have plenty?"

I Hear Ya *also* **I Heard That** *and* **I Heard Ya** A phrase used in response to general statements. Its usage is an informal reaction to statements in conversation to indicate understanding or agreement. Not used to answer a question.

Jeffin' An old expression meaning to tease someone by telling him things that are either untrue or exaggerated.

Jeffin' has expanded to encompass all forms of lying, but it is generally used in a lighter, more humorous vein.

Live *also* **All the Way Live** *and* **Way Live** Happening or exciting. "When I first got on the 'yard' it was all the way live but now there is nothing happening."

Make Me Know It Then A phrase used by inmates daring someone to prove something. Primarily used in jest amongst friends during teasing or jovial bickering; occasionally used as a retort to a threat or provocation.

Mercy Pronounced with exaggeration as *Mur*-say. An exclamatory reply or remark. It replaces "street" expressions like "Oh my" or "My goodness." Used in any circumstance, but most often in stimulating or exciting situations.

On Time Something of exceptional quality is said to be on time. On time is also used to mean something is timely—as in: A glass of ice water after a 5K race is on time.

Same Ol' Same Ol' Short for "same old thing" or "same old shit." Same ol' same ol' is a response to the greeting, "Hi, how are you doing?" Since every day is basically the same in prison, same ol' same ol' means nothing has changed.

Same Shit, Different Day A response to a greeting indicating nothing is new or changed. "Hey Tracy, what's happening?" His reply would be, "Same shit, different day."

Show Me Prove something to someone. It has a dare-like quality. Occasionally used seriously, but usually in jest.

Straight Up Used to indicate that something is the truth.
May also be used to indicate a person is honest and trustworthy. "He is a straight up guy." A straight up convict is one with character. (Archaic: *on the up and up*)

Talking Out of Your Neck *also* **Talking Out the Side of Your Neck** Talking a lot of nonsense or lies. "Hey Neil, try telling the truth and quit talking out of your neck."

That'll Work A general affirmation of a statement. "Hey Fred, I'll pay you back the three dollars tomorrow." The response would be, "That'll work."

That's What's Happenin' The ultimate or absolute best in goods or services. "I'd like to have a brand new, red Corvette convertible. Now that's what's happenin'."

Think It Ain't *also* **Think I Ain't?** *and* **Think It Don't?** Expressions used as general responses to indicate "yes" or "of course" to a particular question or statement. "Your new T.V. works well." The response might be, "Think it don't?"
Think I won't? and think I don't? are similar expressions to those above and are used in a similar style. Think I won't? is a response to a threat, provocation or dare. Think I don't? is a response to a question of ability or capability.

Trick Bag A no-win situation. When a person is placed in an unfavorable and compromising situation, he is said to be placed in a trick bag. An inmate who is involved with a gang may be forced to attack and stab an enemy of the gang. If he does the stabbing, he may get injured or get caught and charged with a new crime. If he does not do it, the gang may avenge this non-complicity by attacking and possibly killing him.

Where He Is Coming From *also* **Where a Person Is Coming From** Used in reference to a person's honesty, integrity and sincerity. "He said he will come back tomorrow to repay the cigarettes he borrowed. We will see then just where he is coming from."

Also used to describe the obnoxious manner in which some inmates occasionally act. "I didn't know where he was coming from when he accused me of stealing his radio."

Black Slang

The slang spoken by black inmates is difficult to capture in a list of words. Black slang has a jazz-like quality and does not conform to set rules but rather has an improvisational feel. Tone, rhythm, loudness and the situation have as much meaning as the words themselves. This makes it impossible to capture the essence of the language on paper. The following words are used in a strictly representative manner.

Ace A good person.

Beat Down A fight amongst inmates. To beat down is to fight.

Blood A name black inmates use amongst themselves when addressing one another. Blood is only used in reference to someone of the same race as it implies unity.

Break Wide To lose interest in a certain situation and leave. Telling someone to break wide is telling him to leave.

Breeze A cool relaxed person.

Cheeb Marijuana.

Chill To loaf or take it easy.

Chilly Most *also* **Chill Out** A calm, relaxed composure with a tranquil state of mind. To become calm and relaxed is to chill out.

Come with It Daring someone to do something.

Crib An inmate's cell or living area.

Cuz *also* **Cuh** A name black inmates use when addressing people during conversation. "Hey cuz, loan me a pack of cigarettes."

Dew Cap *also* **Dew Rag** A plastic cap or bandanna that black inmates use to cover their hair to help retain moisture.

Dog Food A black expression used to mean heroin.

Dog House A protective custody unit.

Fat Nuts An inmate is referred to as having fat nuts when he uses force or intimidation on other inmates. A person with fat nuts is a "bulldogger" and will force a person to do something against his will or take something from him.

Flip A passive homosexual.

Fresh Cut A nice, clean haircut.

Half a Man A passive homosexual.

Having Yourself Masturbation.

Home Boy *also* **Homie** A name blacks call one another in a show of friendship and unity.
    Also used to indicate two people are from the same town, state or geographic region.

Homes A name used to address someone in conversation.

In a Minute A phrase black inmates use when leaving or going somewhere. In a minute is used in place of "goodbye" or "see you later."

Less Than Nothin' A passive homosexual.

Let's Get Busy with It Telling someone to hurry.

Lip Music Black, slang dialogue. One black inmate teases another about losing a domino game and the loser replies, "Turn off that lip music."

Little Joe in the Snow *also* **Blow** Cocaine.

Loose Link An informer.

Master The ultimate or absolute best. Master may refer to people, drugs or a productive way in which a prison sentence is served.

Mix A situation in which the circumstances create an unfavorable and compromising position. Another way in which mix is used is to remember information for future reference. When facts or information about someone or something are recorded in one's memory for future reference, it is referred to as putting that information in the mix.

Money A trusted or best friend.

My Gun Friend.

Nut Role To act crazed or abnormal. A person plays a nut role in certain situations to gain an advantage or achieve a specific goal. "I nut roled on them so they wouldn't put me in isolation." A person who nut roles must be careful not to carry the charade so far that he is placed in the mental ward of the prison.

Poop Butt A distrusted or disreputable person.

Pug A black expression used in reference to a homosexual.

Pull Dude An informer.

Punk's Run A protective custody unit.

Scrub An ignorant individual.

Shake Someone Down *also* **Shake You Down** To have sex with someone. This can be homosexual or heterosexual.

Sherm Another term for PCP. Sherman cigarettes are soaked with the drug PCP, thus the name sherm.

Squeeze *also* **Main Squeeze** Refers to one's girlfriend. Can also mean a good friend or drug connection. "My main squeeze is holdin' the bag. So we be gettin' loaded tonight 'cuz'."

Squeeze *also* **Mr. Whipple** *and* **Bomb** Expressions used in reference to the drug PCP that has been mixed with embalming fluid.

That's Word The absolute truth. That's word refers to truthfulness in speech or writing.

Whack Attack Acting crazed when experiencing the effects of PCP or an hallucinogenic drug.

Word Up "Straight up" or you've got my word on it.

Spanish Slang

The following terms are used primarily by a prison's Spanish population. These are strictly representative.

Bato The English equivalent is dude. "Hey bato, what's happening?"

Bato Loco A crazy dude. Normally used in a joking, friendly manner.

Bonke A prison bunk or bed.

Bote (Pronounced bo-tay.) A county jail. Does not refer to a prison.

Buscale When an inmate comes to your cell trying to borrow something and you tell him buscale, you are telling him to leave and look somewhere else.

Cachero The dominant partner in a homosexual relationship.

Cajita A "box bag" of marijuana.

Calmado Literally means calm or quiet. Used in prison to mean "chill out" or take it easy.

Canton One's cell or house.

Carga Heroin.

Carnal A trusted or good friend.

Chante Literally means house, but in prison it is used to mean a prison cell.

Chava A degrading expression which means that a man is a wimp.

Chingasos A fist fight.

Chirulin (Pronounced cheer-u-lean.) A police informant.

Cholo A member of the same clique or gang. Also a friend or one of the guys.

Chorros *also* **Keep Chorros** A lookout. An inmate keeping watch for prison guards while an illegal activity is taking place is a chorros.
To keep chorros is to be watching for prison guards.

Clavo Someone who is "holding the bag" or the "dope sack." Can also be used to mean holding anything of value, i.e., money, jewels, etc.

Cocer Literally to burn. Cocer refers to death row inmates who are to be executed by electrocution.

Coche Literally means pig, but in prison it refers to a guard.

Compuesto The "fixing" or shooting of drugs, primarily heroin.

Condena A prison term or stretch in prison.

Dedo Literally means finger. A person who puts the finger on someone who has violated prison rules.

Ese (Pronounced es-say.) A term Hispanics use when addressing another Hispanic in conversation. "Hey ese, loan me a pack of cigarettes."

Esquina Refers to partners or "road dogs."

Fileaso (Pronounced fill-a-ah-so.) A knife fight.
Any fight in prison that has knives or "shanks" involved.

Filero Knife or "shank."
Also refers to "hype" or syringe.

Frajos Cigarettes.

Gallina Literally means chicken. A coward.

Joto A homosexual. Although joto is used to mean any homosexual, it is primarily used in reference to the passive partner in a homosexual relationship.

Juras (Pronounced hoo-rras.) A derogatory term used in reference to prison guards, prison authorities or policemen.

Lajua A prison sentence. Sometimes used to mean a life sentence.

Leno (Pronounced lain-yo.) A marijuana cigarette or "joint."

La Ley Literally the law. In prison slang la ley means cop or guard.

La libre Literally means free. A prison expression for the free world or the "streets."

Maricon An inmate who has no courage.

Marimacha A "butch" female. A female who looks and acts like a male and assumes the dominant, active role in a lesbian relationship.

Mi Ruca A convict's wife or girlfriend. The English equivalent is "old lady."

Mota Marijuana.

No Tiene Huevos A slang expression which means "You haven't got any balls."

Pandillas An inmate who will enter another person's cell, while he is there, and boldly take whatever he wants by force.

Pinta Prison.

Pisto Prison-made alcoholic beverages.

Placa Placa means plate or shingle (of a professional person). In prison, placa is the tag or nickname you go by.
Can also be used as a reference to the police.

Printos Inmates or prisoners.

Puto Homosexual.

Quemar Literally to burn or rip off. Refers to an inmate getting "burned" or taken on a drug deal or any deal. When an inmate receives either no drugs or poor quality drugs for money he has paid, it is said he was "burned" or quemar.

Quicas A derogatory term used in reference to a prison guard or policeman.

Quiubo A greeting Hispanics use when seeing one another. It means "hello" or "what's happening?"

Ratero A sneak thief or burglar. A ratero is always watching inmates' cells in hopes of finding one open so he can steal something. A ratero will also break into someone's cell to steal something.

Raton *also* **rata** Literally means rat. A person who "rats" or "snitches" on someone.

Roveche A person who is a thief.

Sancho A man on the "street" who dates or steals an inmate's wife or girlfriend. "When I called home last night, Sancho answered the phone.

Te Sales An individual who does not conform to prison standards.
     Also refers to an inmate who is being released from prison.

Tecato A heroin addict or "junkie."

Tiempo Literally means time. It is used in prison to refer to how much time an inmate is serving on his sentence.

Los Torcidos Literally means the twisted. Hispanics use los torcidos in reference to someone who has been arrested and forced to snitch on his friends or crime partners.

Yesca Marijuana.

Ethnic Slurs

Bones A black person.

Bongo Lips A black person.

Boo Boo's A black person.

Boot Lip A black person.

Breeds A non-white person. The name carries the implication the person is of a mixed racial background.

Chocolate Bar A black person.

Devil A white person.

Fade Term for a white person.

Gavacho A white person.

Generic A non-white person. The name carries the implication the person is not a quality individual.

Grey Boy A white person.

Jap A black person.

Jig A black person.

Jigaboo A black person.

Maggot A white person.

Mayate A black person.

Moon Cricket A black person.

Mud Flap A black person.

Night Fighter A black person.

Off Brand Any non-white person.

Orangutan A black person.

Pack Term for a white person.

Peckerwood A white person.

Pink A white person.

Pink Whoogie Term for a white person.

Porch Monkey A black person.

Prunes A black person.

Rug A black person.

Rug Head A black person.

Sabana A white person.

Scrub A black person.

Spade A black person.

Splib A black person.

Spook A black person.

Titre A black person.

Toad A black person.

Whoogie Term for a white person.

Wood A white person.

Yanta A black person.

Zigaboo A black person.

Zulu A black person.

Transmitting Messages

Burglarize a Conversation When two or more people are having a conversation and someone eavesdrops and butts in with comments or suggestions of his own, he is said to be burglarizing their conversation. This is a dangerous thing to do in prison as everyone's conversations are private and deserve the respect and consideration to remain that way. Inmates take a personal affront to someone burglarizing their conversation, and frequently a fight ensues. (Archaic: *lip in*)

Jungle Jive A term used by women inmates to refer to black rap music.

On the Pipe *also* **Talking on the Pipe** In a cellhouse there is little opportunity for prisoners to conduct private conversations from one cell to another. "Talking on the pipe" is a procedure inmates use enabling them to do this. This is accomplished by the inmates in neighboring cells forcing the water out of their toilet bowls, thereby opening the connecting pipes which allows their voices to travel from one cell to the other. To force the water from the toilet, the inmate in each cell places a pillow or folded blanket on the toilet bowl, sits on it and bounces up and down, creating a plunger effect. Unfortunately, this does not prevent other prisoners in adjoining cells from forcing the water out of their toilets and eavesdropping on the conversation. However, the main purpose is to keep the conversation from the guard's hearing.

Snitch Box *also* **Kite Box** A box in which inmates put institutional correspondence. Often inmates use these boxes to deliver messages about illegal activities of other convicts, hence the name snitch box. (Archaic: *warden's box, dep's box*)

Telegram A written or verbal piece of information that is passed along a cellblock where the men are in a lockdown situation. For example, a message could be sent out the cellblock is going to be flooded and everyone should take their property off the floor and put it up on their bunks.

7

SEXUALITY

Homosexuality

Bitch A name used in jest between homosexuals.
Also used to represent a passive homosexual partner.
(Archaic: *hump*)

Booty Bandit An individual who engages in sex with homosexuals and takes the dominant or male role.

Burning Coal A sexual relationship between a white and black man. Also used to indicate a sexual relationship between women or a heterosexual relationship.

Butch A female who looks and acts like a male and assumes the dominant, active role in a lesbian relationship.

Butt slut A homosexual who takes the passive role.

Catcher The passive partner in a bisexual or homosexual relationship. (Archaic: *stern-wheeler*)

Chicken A young, pretty homosexual. Although any young, pretty homosexual is considered a chicken, it is used more often in reference to blond ones. (Archaic: *brat*)

Chicken Hawk A bisexual or homosexual who seeks relationships with young attractive men. (Archaic: *uncle, gash hound*)

Cum Chum A passive homosexual.

Cup Cakes A homosexual, primarily a passive one. (Archaic: *fruit*)

Dad *also* **Daddy** A homosexual's lover, who owns or controls him. In prison, most passive, feminine homosexuals are owned or controlled by the stronger inmates. A homosexual's dad is generally "straight" or bisexual and has a responsibility to protect and support him. Much of the trouble that occurs in prison is due to inmates fighting over "queens." A homosexual's dad must always be prepared to fight to protect and retain possession of his "kid." (Archaic: *papa*)

Donut Bumper Dominant lesbian inmate.

Douche Bag *also* **Slut Puppy** Refer to a woman who has sexual relations with many other women. Used in a contemptuous manner. "That douche bag has slept with nearly every woman on the 'yard'."

Fag *also* **Faggot** A homosexual. Used to signify both dominant and passive homosexual partners. (Archaic: *piece of snatch, hunk of hat*)

Fem An individual who takes on the female role in a homosexual relationship.

Flip Flop To have sex with both men and women. A bisexual person is said to flip flop.
   Also used to indicate a homosexual who engages in both the active and passive roles in a homosexual relationship. A homosexual who flip flops will "pitch" and "catch."

Fudge Packer A person who takes the male role in anal sex with another inmate.

Girl A feminine, passive homosexual. (Archaic: *nola, ring tail*)

He-she A passive homosexual.

Hole A passive, feminine homosexual. A hole usually does not belong to one particular individual, but rather, has sex with many different men. (Archaic: *fruit for monkeys*)

Home Grown *also* **Stud Broad** Used in reference to "butch" females.

Husband The dominant partner in a homosexual relationship. The dominant partner in prison relationships may be homosexual but is usually bisexual and has sex with men because women are unavailable.

Kid A passive homosexual partner. A person's kid is his "punk." In prison, most passive homosexuals are owned or controlled by stronger inmates. (Archaic: *kife*)

Lezzie A lesbian is called a "lezzie."

Mud Packer A person who takes the dominant role in a homosexual relationship.

Pile Driver A person who takes the dominant role in a homosexual relationship.

Pitcher The dominant or active partner in a bisexual or homosexual relationship. (Archaic: *keister bandit*)

Pole Pleaser A passive homosexual.

Punk One of the oldest and most widely used terms signifying a homosexual. Although punk is used to mean any homosexual, it is primarily used to indicate the passive partner in a homosexual relationship.
Punk is also used as a verb. To punk someone is to sexually penetrate him. (Archaic: *gunzel*)

Queen An extremely feminine, passive homosexual. (Archaic: *candy, gash*)

Semen Demon A homosexual who takes the passive role.

Sister An affectionate term used among homosexuals. There is a considerable amount of jealousy between some homosexuals and sister is only used between friends.

Sweet Kid *also* **Sweet Meat** A young and pretty, passive homosexual partner. (Archaic: *apple pie*)

Turned Out *also* **Turn a Person Out** Changing a person's sexual habits from heterosexual to homosexual. A person may be turned out by force or persuasion. Many young men coming to prison are immediately subjected to homosexuality. Some of these men enjoy it or are physically unable to refuse. "He was turned out when he was 19 and he has been a 'fag' ever since." (Archaic: *made fag, made gunzel*)

Twinkie A passive homosexual.

Undercover Fag *also* **Closet Queen** A man who tries to keep his homosexuality a secret from the majority of the prison population.

Wolf A bisexual or dominant homosexual partner. (Archaic: *turk*)

Body Parts

Bearded Clam The vagina.

Bone The penis.

Bone Phone The penis.

Butt Pussy The anus.

Chinchilla The vagina.

Gash The vagina.

Hershey Highway The anus. "Bob took a ride on the hershey highway."

Hinie Hideout The anus.

Hinie Highway The anus.

Johnson The penis.

Kitty The vagina.

Knob The penis.

McMuff The vagina.

Meat Whistle The penis.

Monkey The vagina.

O-Ring The anus.

One-eyed Trouser Snake The penis.

One-eyed Worm The penis.

Pant Worm The penis.

Pink Eye The vagina.

Poop Chute The anus.

Red Snapper The vagina.

Rocky Road The anus.

Round Pussy The anus.

The Safe The anus.

Schlong The penis.

Slash The vagina.

Slice The vagina.

Slit The vagina.

Snapper The vagina.

The Suitcase The anus.

Third Eye The anus.

The Tomb The anus.

Trouser Trout The penis. "How about some trouser trout smothered in shorts?"

Whammer The penis.

Sexual Acts

Bone Down Copulation with a female.

Bone Gobbler Someone who performs oral sex.

Bumper Head Someone who performs oral sex.

Choke the Chicken Masturbation. (Archaic: *beat the bishop*)

Clean the Pipe The act of oral sex.

Fifi Bag Some type of bag or container which is filled with a lubricant and used to masturbate.

Flog the Log Masturbation. (Archaic: *beat the dummy*)

Head Hunter One who performs oral sex.

Hide the Salami Copulation with a woman.

Hose Sex with a woman.

Kill Some Babies To masturbate. (Archaic: *kick the gong around*)

Knock the Dust Off the Old Sombrero The act of oral sex.

Lip Action *also* **Lip Dancin'** *and* **Lip Music** Two men kissing each other.
    Also used to mean oral sex.

Packin' Mud An expression for anal intercourse. "Phil has been packin' mud all weekend."

Peter Puffer One who performs oral sex.

Polish the Knob The act of oral sex.

Polish the Old German Helmet Oral sex.

Pull the Chain Masturbation. (Archaic: *flog the pork*)

Pullin' the Pud Masturbation. (Archaic: *snap the rubber*)

Put Some Slobber on the Knobber The act of oral sex.

Shot of Crack Sex with a female.

Skull Oral sex.

Swappin' Spit Two men kissing each other.
    Also used to mean oral sex. (Archaic: *swap spits*)

Yankin' the Crank Masturbation. (Archaic: *snap the whip*)

8

CIGARETTES & FOOD

Cigarettes

Cigarettes are the basic medium of exchange in prison. They are used to purchase everything from illegal drugs to sexual favors. Prison prices are quoted in packs of cigarettes, not in dollars and cents. Such services as laundry, hair cuts and ironing are normally paid for with packs of cigarettes to ensure the job is done well. It should be noted that cigarettes, as used in this context, mean name brand or "tailor made" cigarettes not generic brands.

Most prison "yards" have a number of individuals who act as a "store" and loan cigarettes and other "store" items for a high interest rate. The standard payback is two packs for every one borrowed. If you miss a week, the payback is four packs for every one borrowed.

Even if an individual does not smoke, he can easily convert cigarettes into other store items that are needed or pay for personal services with them. It is because of this versatility that cigarettes are used as prison currency.

Box One carton or ten packs of cigarettes. A box of premium cigarettes is the prison equivalent of $15.

G's *also* **Plain Wrapper** Generic, manufactured cigarette.
Generic cigarettes are used as a medium of exchange but on a lesser scale than "premiums." G's have about one-half the value of "premiums."

Premiums Name brand cigarettes are called premiums. Only name brand, manufactured cigarettes can be premiums, not generics or "roll-ees."

Ready Mades Hand-rolled cigarettes that are pre-rolled.

Rock A prison dollar, equivalent to one pack of name brand cigarettes. In every society there is a medium of exchange. In prison, inmates are not allowed to have currency, so the most common means used for the acquisition of products and services is cigarettes.

Rollie A hand-rolled cigarette. Rollies are made with loose tobacco and individual rolling papers and rolled by hand or a hand-rolling machine. Rollies are never used in prison as money.

Rollie also refers to all the materials necessary to make a hand-rolled cigarette. (Archaic: *makin's*)

Running a Store All prison yards have inmates who run a store. This means he keeps cigarettes, sodas, candy, etc. in stock in his cell and loans it out for profit. The normal interest rate is two for one and can run as high as three for one. This practice is illegal and often leads to problems. If a person does not make payment, the store owner may use physical violence in retaliation.

Shorts The last one-third to one-fourth of a cigarette. To save someone shorts on a cigarette is to save him a couple of draws at the end.

Snipe A re-smokeable cigarette butt. A snipe can be any kind of cigarette butt, whether manufactured or hand-rolled, which has enough tobacco left so that it can be re-lit and smoked again. (Archaic: *lipburner, dincher, clincher*)

Square A manufactured cigarette. The term square originates from the fact that a regular cigarette does not cause its user to become "high." (Archaic: *pill*)

Straight A seldom used term to indicate a manufactured cigarette. Straight is derived from the fact that the user remains "straight" when smoking, and does not get "stoned."

Tailor Made *also* **Tailor** *and* **TM's** A manufactured cigarette, whether it is a name brand or generic.

Food

Food is also used as a bartering tool. Since prison food is usually of a poor quality and lacks any kind of appeal, the food that is used for trading or for payments is store bought. It is normally junk food such as chips, candy, soda, cakes and pies.

Beagles Old term for sausages.

Bomb *also* **Bomb and Cooker** In county jails and most prisons, inmates are provided with only the necessities for their basic needs such as food, shelter and hygienic products. Prisoners can be quite inventive when they do not have conventional means to do even the most common and ordinary things, such as heating water or coffee. A "bomb" is a source of heat whereby inmates roll toilet paper into a tight coil and set it afire. This is accomplished by wrapping many layers of toilet paper around one's hand making a dense roll. The bomb is then placed on the back of the toilet and set afire. The more layers of toilet paper used the longer the bomb will burn. To extinguish the fire, the bomb is simply knocked into the toilet bowl. The cooker is the container used to heat the water over the fire. An aluminum soft drink can is usually used to make the cooker, and a wet washcloth or sock is used to hold the cooker to prevent burning the hand.

Bug *also* **Stinger** An electrical device that heats water. Most bugs are used to heat water one cup at a time for coffee or tea. In some prisons, inmates are not allowed to have hot pots or coffee pots and stingers are the only way to heat water.

Bull *also* **Mountain Goat** Old term for meat.

Chow Prison food. There are relatively few terms describing prison food. (Archaic: *gooby, gullion, slumgullion, slum*)

Chow Hall Prison dining room. (Archaic: *mess hall*)

Death Loaf Meat loaf.

Flit *also* **Mouthwash, Spow** Old term for coffee.

Fried Rubber Fried liver.

Grease Patties Chicken fried steak.

Hollywood Stew Old term for creamed codfish.

Judy *also* **Jupe Balls** The name for the meals that are served in the "hole" or lockdown areas. This meal is part of the punishment. Judy is a ground patty 4″ × 4″ × 3″ and is made up of the entire meal's ingredients which have been run through a grinder. They are traditionally served burned on the outside and raw on the inside.

Jug Up To eat a prison meal. "They just announced the supper line. Let's go jug up." (Archaic: *Chuck, graze, scorf*)

Monkey Nuts Meat balls.

Mulligan Old term for stew.

Nigger-Heads Old term for prunes.

Nux Old term for tea.

Pigeon *also* **Yard-Bird** Fried chicken.

Piss 'n' Punk (Old expression) Rations of bread and water which are served in the "hole" or lockdown areas. This practice is not as widespread today. (Archaic: *angel cake & wine*)

Punk *also* **Dummy, Double-O** Bread.

Red Death Barbeque beef or pork.

Sand Sugar.

Shrubbery Old term for sauerkraut.

Soy Pucks Hamburgers.

Spa-Gag-Me Prison spaghetti. (Archaic: *lead pipe*)

Store Any item purchased from or available at the inmate store.

Wham Whams Store-bought snacks.

Zoo Zoos Sweet snacks, cookies or potato chips. This term is generally used to indicate snacks purchased from or available at the inmate store.

9

DRUGS & ALCOHOL

Types

Angel Dust A term used to denote the drug PCP. PCP is a strong and unpredictable hallucinogenic drug, and one of its more dangerous characteristics is causing its user to experience temporary losses of consciousness. During these periods of blackout, the drug user is likely to commit acts he normally would not do. This is reflected within the prison population as there are many individuals serving time for crimes committed while under the influence of this drug.

Blow A term used in reference to cocaine. It is derived from the inhaling or "snorting" manner in which cocaine is ingested.

Boy Heroin. "He is loaded on that boy again."

China White A pure, snow white heroin in powder form. It was originally made exclusively in China and distributed throughout Asia. However, it is now made throughout the Orient. In the 1960s and 1970s, this was the best form of heroin available. (Archaic: *white stuff*)

Chocolate Stuff *also* **Chocolate** Mexican heroin. Mexican heroin is prevalent in prison.

D's The most common name for Dilaudid. It is a synthetic, pharmaceutically produced opiate closely resembling heroin.

Down Heroin.

Girl Cocaine. "He is snorting that girl."

Hootch *also* **Brew** *and* **Home Brew** Terms used to indicate any type of homemade alcoholic beverage. Also used to indicate legal, manufactured liquor that has been smuggled into the prison.

Horse *also* **Shag** *and* **Stuff** Heroin. Of the three terms, stuff is more widely used in prison to mean heroin. (Archaic: *H, majonda*)

Ice A new form of amphetamine that is sold in solid form in ice-like crystals. It is cheap and extremely addictive. The high lasts much longer than that produced by cocaine.

Idiot Juice A nutmeg and water combination used in prison as an intoxicant.
      Idiot juice may also be used to indicate any prison-made alcoholic beverage.

Jack *also* **Raisin Jack, Apple Jack** *and* **Pruno** Prison-made wines.

Juice A catch-all term used to mean any type of alcoholic beverage, whether it is homemade or manufactured.

Kicker A small amount of homemade wine that is rich in yeast cultures and is used to start the fermentation process in a fresh batch of fruit juice and sugar (hootch).

Mash All the ingredients used to make "hootch," such as fruit pulp, raisins or potatoes. Mash includes everything but the liquid.

Mexican Mud *also* **Mud** Mexican heroin. When "China white" heroin became scarce in the early to mid–1970s, it was replaced by Mexican heroin. Mexican heroin was cheaper and more readily available which enabled its popularity to rapidly increase. This heroin is brown in color and forms a brown liquid when mixed with water and cooked.

Opiate Derived from or containing opium or one of its derivatives. Opium and its derivatives are processed from the poppy plant, so an opiate is any drug originating from the poppy plant. This includes heroin, morphine, and opium.

Pot *also* **Grass** *and* **Smoke** Marijuana. (Archaic: *yen-pop, gonga*)

Ree-Faahh A variation of the word reefer. This exaggerated pronunciation is more prevalent in prison.

Reefer Marijuana. (Archaic: *gage*)

Rock *also* **Crack** A form of cocaine, refined and processed into chunks or rocks to be smoked in a glass pipe device. This form of using cocaine is referred to as "free-base" or "free-basing" and became popular in the 1980s.
  Originally, rock referred to the rock crystal type of cocaine. When cocaine is manufactured, the last stage of the refining process leaves the drug in a rock crystal form. It is then ground into a powder form.

Scrap Iron A drink made with rubbing alcohol, mothballs and a chlorine solution which has intoxicating properties.

Sherm A street name given to PCP.

Tootsie Roll *also* **Tar** Mexican heroin. It is called tootsie roll because of the fact this form of heroin is dark brown and sticky and resembles Tootsie Roll candy.

Wacky Backy A term used to indicate marijuana. It is primarily used by the country 'n' western or cowboy population of the prison.

Administration

Dusted To have consumed and finished an amount of any drug. "I just dusted off that last 'bag' of weed."

Fix To inject a drug intravenously or "shoot" it.
  The term fix originated when a drug user would take a powdered drug, usually heroin, pour the powder into a spoon, add water, cook and mix until all the powder had dissolved. The liquid would be drawn into a needle and

syringe through cotton or a cigarette filter for straining and then injected intravenously. This entire process was called fixing dope. The actual act of injecting the drug is called "shooting." Fixing dope is now generally referred to as the actual injection or the "shooting" of the drug. This is primarily due to the recent increase of liquid pharmaceutical drugs that require no preparation, or easily mixed powder drugs that require little preparation.

Fix My Bones *also* **Do Something for My Bones** An expression used primarily by narcotic addicts meaning to give them a "fix." It is common for addicts going into withdrawals to have aching bones and this is what the expression refers to. "I'm really hurtin', why don't you fix my bones?"

Hit The actual injecting of the drug. "Will you hit me?"
     A hit is also used as a reference to smoking marijuana that means a "toke" or draw off a marijuana cigarette. "Take a hit off this joint."

Roller A vein that is difficult to use in intravenous drug injection due to the fact that it rolls from side to side. "Don't hit that vein, it is a roller."

Runnin' The act of shooting narcotics over a period of time. "Fred has been runnin' 'junk' for days."

Scratch Your Monkey *also* **Feed Your Monkey** The daily "shooting" of drugs to satisfy a person's habit. The correlation with scratching is that the drug habit is a continuous itch that needs to be scratched. The more you scratch, or the more drugs you do, the more it itches, or the more drugs you need. To feed your monkey is to do enough of the drug to keep your habit from making you sick through withdrawal.

Shoot To inject drugs intravenously. (Archaic: *shot in the arm*)

Shotgun A powerful and explosive way to smoke a marijuana cigarette. This is accomplished by lighting a joint in the conventional manner, making sure it is burning evenly and briskly, then placing the lit end inside your mouth ensuring the fire does not hit your tongue or the inside of your mouth. You then place your lips around the joint in an airtight fashion, position the other end several inches in front of a person's face and blow forcefully. This will produce a powerful stream of smoke which comes out the other end. The receiver of the smoke inhales as much as possible. This will produce a more intense "high" and it can be achieved in less time than the conventional manner of smoking marijuana. (Archaic: *bang a reefer*)

Slammin' *also* **Slam** When a person is using drugs by intravenous injection, he is said to be slammin'. "He 'copped' some heroin this morning and he has been slammin' all day." (Archaic: *bang*)

Smoke One Smoking a marijuana cigarette. "Hey, let's go smoke one." (Archaic: *blow one's roof*)

Sniff Intoxicating substances ingested by inhalation (i.e., paint thinner, gasoline and glue).

Wake-Up The dose of drugs addicts have saved from the previous day to ensure a morning "fix." It should be noted a wake-up is not always available. Most addicts live from fix to fix and often consume all of their supply without saving anything for the next day.

Measurement

Bag *also* **Sack** Terms loosely used to mean various quantities of drugs. These may be used to represent any type drug but generally refer to marijuana or drugs in powder form.

    The terms dope sack and dope bag are used to indicate a person is still using drugs. "He is still in the dope bag" or "He cannot get out of the dope sack."

Box A box refers to one carton or ten packs of cigarettes. Cigarettes are the most common medium of exchange in prison, being used to buy everything from drugs to services or favors.

    The term box also means a unit of measure associated with marijuana. In the 1950s and 1960s, before marijuana became so expensive, it was sold in matchboxes for about ten dollars. Although buying marijuana is still sometimes referred to as buying a "matchbox," in reality, ten dollars will only buy about a sewing thimble full of marijuana in prison.

Box Bag A popular method by which drugs, primarily marijuana, are sold in prison. This refers to the amount of marijuana a person can buy for one carton of cigarettes or approximately ten dollars. This is usually one, small thimble full, enough for three "pinrolled" marijuana cigarettes.

Cap A unit of measure equalling one dose of a drug. A cap may also be used as a unit of measure of marijuana. A method now being used in prison is filling the inside of a toothpaste cap with marijuana and selling this amount as a "box bag" or a ten dollar "bag" of marijuana. This small amount would equal approximately three "pinrolled joints." "Sell me a cap of reefer."

Dem Things *also* **Them Things** Marijuana cigarettes. As in: "Why don't we smoke one of dem things?" (Archaic: *roach*)

Fix One dose or injection of an intravenous drug. It is usually dispensed dry but it may be pre-mixed into a liquid form and drawn into a syringe.

Fold A paper that is folded in such a way as to keep the drugs it contains from falling out. Illegal substances are often sold in units of measure called "papers" or folds. A standard price for a fold is $25.

Hit One dose or injection of a drug—"Give me a hit of heroin."

Hooter Another name for a marijuana cigarette. This term is popular in southwestern prisons. (Archaic: *goof butt*)

Joint *also* **Number** A marijuana cigarette. Since marijuana is expensive and often difficult to obtain in prison, a joint is always extremely small. (Archaic: *muggles*)

Line A small marijuana cigarette. Line is also a dose of cocaine. While cocaine is found in prisons, it is not as prevalent as heroin or marijuana. This is probably due to the fact that the "high" from cocaine is so short-lived and the drug is so expensive.

Paper *also* **Quarter Paper** Paper refers to a unit of measure of drugs in powder form, usually heroine or cocaine. These drugs are sold in slick finish or cellophane paper as it will not absorb any of the drug. The most common size paper is the 25-dollar paper called a quarter paper.

Papers are also referred to as "good" or "nice" meaning the amount and quality are good for the price. Consequently, "bad" would mean the opposite. (Archaic: *piece*)

Pinroll *also* **Pinrolled Joint** *and* **Pinner** Used to indicate the small size of a marijuana cigarette. Because marijuana is so scarce and expensive in prison, inmates tend to smoke the smallest amount possible that can be rolled in cigarette form.

Quarter Bag *also* **Quarter Sack** A bag or sack of drugs costing $25. In prison, dollar amounts are referred to as coin amounts. A nickel is $5, a dime is $10 and 50 cents is $50. The most popular size quantity of "hard" drugs, such as heroine and cocaine, is the quarter bag or 25-dollar "paper."

Spoon Originally, a spoon was used to cook and mix heroin in preparation for an injection. Since this was almost always one dose or "hit," it has since come to mean a unit of measure of one dose of a drug, primarily a drug that is "shot" or injected, such as heroin.

Acquisition

Balloon A common means of smuggling drugs into prison. This can be accomplished in several ways. Using ordinary children's balloons, a person takes several small balloons and inserts them inside each other making three or four layers. These balloons are then filled with drugs, tied and sealed. They are smuggled into a visitation area of the prison, usually in a woman's bra or wig, and are passed to the inmate. The inmate has a choice of several ways of smuggling these balloons out of the visitation area and back to the cellhouses. This is usually accomplished by swallowing the balloons and retrieving them later either by regurgitation or waiting a day or two and removing them from the feces. If this latter method is used, special attention must be given to the substance of which the balloons are made as the body's digestive juices will erode some balloon substances and release the drugs-into the body. Another means of smuggling balloons into prison is by inserting them into a person's anus in a suppository manner and retrieving them later.

Clean A person not in possession of any drugs as well as not using drugs.

Clean may be used in reference to any contraband or illegal activity to indicate the person in question is not involved in any such activities.

Dirty Indicates a person is in possession of, or "holding," drugs as well as using drugs.

Dirty may be used in reference to any contraband or illegal activity.

Holdin' To have drugs in one's possession. This can mean the individual has drugs for his personal use or for sale.

Keyster Literally, keyster refers to a person's buttocks. This is the name given to smuggling or placing something in a person's anus. To smuggle drugs in one's anus would be to keyster them. Weapons and other things can also be hidden in a person's anus.

The Safe *also* **The Suitcase** A person's anus. It is used as a means of smuggling drugs into a prison. Drugs are wrapped in balloons or plastic wrap and sealed very tightly, then lubricated and inserted into the anus. The term safe came about because inmates keep contraband items secured there during "shakedowns" or while transporting them.

Street to Street *also* **Send Out** A popular method of buying drugs in prison. This is accomplished by having someone on the "street" send payment to another "street" address for drugs received in prison. This method is primarily used for quantities of drugs costing $25 or more.

Send out is also used in reference to an inmate who sends money from his account from the prison to a "street" address. This method is rarely used as it stimulates suspicion, and many prisons do not allow inmates to send money to private "street" addresses.

Effects

Blazed High on marijuana. (Archaic: *gaged*)

Cop a Nod *also* **Coppin' a Nod** To get "stoned" or "loaded" on heroin or Dilaudid. This phrase is also used to describe someone who has just injected heroin. (Archaic: *junked up*)

Dump *also* **Lunch Gut** When "shooting" or injecting the drug Dilaudid or a good quality heroin, most people become nauseated and vomit within the first few minutes. This does not last long and it is called dumping or spilling your lunch guts. Most drug addicts enjoy this dumping as they go from vomiting to being extremely euphoric within a few minutes.

Habit An addiction. Although an addiction may be physical, psychological or both, habit is used in conjunction with physical addiction and generally associated with the drugs heroin, Dilaudid or some opiate drug. When a person first starts using drugs, a euphoric feeling is easily achieved with a small amount of the drug. As the usage continues, however, the amount of the drug needed to achieve this euphoric "high" rapidly increases until the point of a habit is reached. When someone has reached this point of drug dependency, the amount of the drug he is doing each time has increased to five or ten times the amount of early usage, and the person is no longer achieving a euphoric state. He is satisfying his habit, but only to the point of not becoming ill. To clarify this point, once the habit stage is reached, the body needs and craves the drug. If after a certain period of time, usually three to eight hours, the body does not receive the drug, it reacts in a negative fashion by making the addict extremely ill. This is called withdrawal. When drug usage has reached the habit stage, it has evolved from recreational use and enjoyment to the single most important necessity of a person's life.

In the Spoon *also* **Out of the Spoon** When an intravenous drug user is using drugs. Although this expression is used to mean any intravenous drug user, it is primarily used to indicate heroin addicts.

A former drug user who is no longer "shooting" drugs is said to be out of the spoon.

Jacked Up A state of being extremely high on drugs. "Kent is really jacked up on cocaine."

Jones *also* **Jonesin'** Withdrawal from a drug habit, especially heroin. "He is really sick, he must be jonesin'." The terms jones and jonesin' are used more often in prison than the term withdrawal.

Kick *also* **Kickin'** *and* **Kickin' the Habit** A traumatic period of withdrawal from drugs until an addict overcomes his addiction—this period of withdrawal is referred to as kickin' or kickin' the habit. An addict may make reference to the fact he is going to kick.

Kickin' may be accomplished several ways, the most severe being "cold turkey." "Cold turkey" means the addict suddenly stops using the drug completely and does not use any substitute drug to aid in the kickin'. This is the most common means of kickin' in prison as the drug supply is in a constant state of fluctuation. Another means of kickin' is the tapering method whereby the addict will do ever smaller, less frequent injections eventually tapering off to nothing. This method will make the withdrawal period less severe. One of the most popular means of kickin' the habit is the Methadone program. Methadone is a synthetic, pharmaceutically produced drug used by drug addicts as a substitute for heroin, Dilaudid or opiates. (Archaic: *kill a Chinaman*)

Loaded *also* **Stoned** Experiences the effects of a particular drug. (Archaic: *charged up*)

Monkey *also* **Monkey on Your Back** When persons are physically addicted to drugs, usually dilaudid, heroin or some other opiate, they are said to have a monkey or monkey on their back. These terms are used to indicate a drug addict's habit, which is the monkey.

Nod *also* **Noddin', Scratch a Nod** *and* **Scratch and Nod** Used to describe someone "stoned" or "loaded" on heroin. When someone gets "loaded" on heroin, noddin' or a momentary loss of consciousness is a typical behavioral characteristic. (Archaic: *on the nod*)

Overamped To overdose on amphetamines or cocaine.

Smacked Back To be high on heroin. (Archaic: *spending a night on a rainbow*)

Strung Out When a person is addicted to drugs, either physically or psychologically, he is said to be strung out. The more addicted a person is the more strung out he becomes.

Another usage of the phrase strung out is in reference to someone who has been using a stimulant (diet pills or cocaine) for several days or weeks and has a disheveled appearance. This person would be strung out in appearance but not necessarily physically addicted to the drug being used. A person may be strung out on almost any drug, including alcohol, but generally it refers to "speed freaks." People who use "speed" or stimulant drugs are referred to as "speed freaks." (Archaic: *up against it*)

Thorazine Shuffle In an institutional environment there are inmates who are violent or afflicted with mental disorders. The prescribed solution to this problem is large doses of tranquilizer drugs, primarily thorazine. While under the influence of thorazine, inmates tend to move in a trance-like stupor. These inmates are referred to as doing the thorazine shuffle.

Wired for Sound To be extremely high on amphetamines or cocaine. (Archaic: *caught in a snow storm*)

Withdrawal In any form of drug addiction, the body and mind are constantly craving the drug to which they are addicted. If for any reason the body does not receive this drug within a period of three to eight hours, it will react in a violent fashion making the drug addict extremely ill. This is called withdrawal. Some withdrawal symptoms are fever, chills, vomiting and dry heaves, headache, crawling skin and insomnia. Withdrawal may be psychological as well as physical. Although psychological withdrawal is not as violent as physical withdrawal, it may be extremely painful and more difficult to overcome in the long run since it does not appear after a few days.

Paraphernalia

Binky A type of modified syringe for the administration of narcotics (*see* **fit**).

Biz The paraphernalia a drug user utilizes to inject heroin and other drugs. A person's "biz" usually consists of a hypodermic needle and syringe, a spoon, a tie-off or tourniquet, cotton and matches.

Cap During the 1950s and 1960s, a soft drink or beer bottle cap was sometimes used as a replacement for a spoon in the cooking and mixing of heroin in preparation for an injection. The cork or rubber liner was removed to allow for the drug and water. The bottle cap was then held by some device while the liquid was being cooked. This was generally some type of heat dissipating material so it would not get too hot to hold, eliminating the possibility of dropping and spilling the drug. The term cap later expanded to mean a unit of measure equalling one dose of a drug.

Fit Originally called Outfit, the term refers to the needle and syringe a person uses to inject drugs intravenously. This includes all types of needles and syringes. The most popular, in recent years, is the plastic, disposable, insulin syringe.

This is a one-piece syringe with a 26 gauge needle permanently attached to one end or imbedded in the plastic "barrel" of the syringe. The part of the syringe that houses the plunger and holds the drug ready for injection is called the "barrel." The "barrel" has measuring numbers on the side that will usually measure up to one c.c. of liquid.

There are two other insulin syringes that have become scarce as they are being replaced by the cheaper, one piece, disposable syringe. They are the plastic syringe with 25 or 26 gauge disposable needles that are separate from the syringe and must be placed on the end of the syringe when being used, and the glass syringe with separate disposable needles. This type of fit consists of a glass "barrel" or syringe part with a plunger inserted inside the "barrel," and comes with individually wrapped, disposable needles that are placed on the end of the "barrel" when being used. This is the preferred outfit with drug users as the glass syringe is more durable and easier to clean and sterilize.

One of the original outfits used by drug addicts was the eye dropper fit. It is made by taking an eye dropper with a rubber compression tip and placing a disposable needle on the end. The drug is drawn and injected by squeezing the rubber tip. With most eye droppers, the tip has to be slightly enlarged to accommodate the needle. This is accomplished by layers of tape or, preferably, layers of thread made hard by being coated with clear nail polish or glue. From this type fit evolved the "binky" or "bopper" type fit employing the eye-dropper principle. This fit utilizes the glass "barrel" or syringe part of a glass fit with the plunger removed. Upon one end is placed the disposable needle as in the glass syringe fit, but the drug is drawn and injected by a "bopper" or "binky" compression procedure very similar to the way an eye dropper works. The "binky" bulb tip is generally made of some type of rubber, artificial fruit, such as a grape or a cherry, but it can be anything rubber or flexible, airtight and with a hole in which to place the glass syringe. This rubber bulb is placed on the syringe at the opposite end of the needle and sealed by wrapping thread or a rubber band around the rubber portion of the "binky" that is making contact with the "barrel" of the syringe.

This is a popular outfit with drug addicts as it tends to lend a certain degree of individualism and "registers" automatically. To "register" is to ensure the needle is in the vein. This is accomplished by drawing a small amount of blood into the syringe prior to injecting the drug. (Archaic: *hype stick*)

Rig Rig is another name for fit or outfit. (Archaic: *banger*)

Slide A syringe that utilizes a plunger type mechanism to inject the drug.

Spoon A spoon or similar object used to cook and mix narcotics in preparation for an injection.

With the rapid increase in the use of cocaine, a small spoon is sometimes used to "snort" or inhale cocaine. This device is called a cocaine or "coke" spoon and it is basically one dose per spoon per nostril.

Tie-Off *also* **Tie** A device used in a tourniquet fashion to enlarge a person's vein making it stand out and move close to the skin surface. This enables the drug user to easily penetrate the skin and vein for a quicker and easier injection. A frequently used tie is a person's belt. A bootlace, leather strap or an extension cord can also be used.

Works *also* **Kit** All the necessary utensils needed to use drugs intravenously. This includes a small spoon, used to mix, liquefy and cook (when needed) the drug; cotton, used to filter the liquid when drawing it into the syringe; a needle and syringe and some type of tie-off such as a belt or boot lace used as a tourniquet. Although these things are the essentials, a person's works may also include some type of object used to mix the drug into a smooth liquid form, but most people use the protective cap or covering of the needle for this purpose; an extremely tiny "spoon" or other object used to measure and put the drug into the "spoon"; and a lighter or matches used to cook and boil the drug in the spoon.

Not all drugs need to be cooked. Drugs such as heroin, Dilaudid and barbituates (sleeping pills and depressants) need to be cooked and lightly boiled as this aids in mixing and removes some of the impurities from the drug. Cocaine and speed (diet pills and stimulants) do not need to be cooked as this decreases the potency of the drug, but a person may want to put a little light heat on these drugs when mixing with water to aid in dissolving the drug. Occasionally, a person will refer to his needle and syringe as his works, but it is generally used to mean one's entire "kit."

Sharing Drugs

Bogart When two or more people are smoking marijuana from the same "joint," it is a normal practice to take a "toke" or draw and pass it to the next person to smoke. When a person takes two or more tokes before passing the joint," or just holds it too long allowing the joint to burn wastefully, he is said to be bogarting the joint. When a person does this selfish practice consistently, he is said to be a bogart. It is generally believed this term originated by the manner in which Humphrey Bogart smoked his cigarettes by always having one in his mouth. The term bogart has since expanded to encompass all forms of selfishness.

The Car *also* **In the Car** *and* **Out of the Car** A group of several inmates who get together to do drugs, usually marijuana. Most always, the car consists of a group of friends. If a person is on friendly terms with these inmates and does drugs or other illegal activities with them, he is said to be in the car. If for some reason an inmate falls from grace with the group and is no longer invited to do drugs with them, he is said to be out of the car.

Carry *also* **Carried** Often when friends do drugs together, there will be times when one does not have the money or resources to obtain his own drugs and will have to rely on his friends to supply him. His friends would be referred to as carrying him. A person can carry another person in many ways, by supplying him with money, cigarettes, drugs, or anything of value. In general, when one person helps another, he is said to be carrying him. This type of favor usually entails a large payback.

Clean A person with negative urinalysis results.

Dirty A person with positive urinalysis results.

Drivin' *also* **Drivin' the Car** When several inmates get together to do drugs, the person who is furnishing the drugs is said to be drivin' the car.

Hitchin' *also* **Hitchhike, Hitch a Ride** *and* **Getting a Free Ride** Refers to someone who is using drugs furnished by someone else rather than paying for them himself. If someone was "in the car" and did not pay for the drugs he was using, he would be hitchin' or getting a free ride. The supplier of the drugs for "the car" would be "drivin'" and everyone else would be hitchhiking.

Pee-Train A woman is on the pee-train when a urine sample is taken from her for analysis to detect drug use.

Ua *also* **Urinalysis** *and* **Piss Test** A routine laboratory test performed on a person's urine to detect drugs or alcohol. The test is frequently performed on prison inmates and people on parole to detect drug use.

10

TATTOOS

Cap A toothpaste cap or thimble full of tattoo ink. If someone is applying a tattoo and runs out of ink before finishing, he would borrow a cap of ink from another tattooist.

Political Tats Tattoos that represent gang insignias or gang membership.
Political tats are also worn by individuals who are not members of gangs. These individuals wear political tats to show rebellion or convey a certain message.

Slingin' Ink *also* **Sling Ink** The application of a tattoo.

Tat *also* **Tack** Short for tattoo. It is the actual drawing etched in ink into someone's skin.

Tat Gun *also* **Gun** The device a "tat man" uses to apply tattoos.

Tat Man *also* **Tat Artist** Someone who applies tattoos on people. Tattooing is a delicate art.

Tat Motor A device used to operate a "tat gun." A "tat motor" can be a device manufactured solely for the purpose of tattooing. In prison, however, it is usually made from some electrical device such as a cassette tape player motor.

Tat Needle The object that actually punctures the skin, to imbed ink, when applying a tattoo. The tat needle is used in conjunction with a "tat gun." In prison, small pieces of guitar strings are used as tat needles.

With the AIDS outbreak, tattooists and people receiving tattoos take as many precautions as possible to reduce their risk of getting this deadly disease. Sharing the same tat needle is a common means by which AIDS is spread. Therefore, people receiving tattoos try to avoid using previously used tat needles. A popular practice in prison is to keep an entire guitar string for one's personal use as a tat needle. A small section is cut from the guitar string and is used every time a person receives a tattoo.

Tat Pattern A printed design or drawing a "tat man" uses as a guide when tattooing someone. In prison, carbon paper, mimeograph, or spirit master paper is used to transfer the tat pattern onto someone's skin. A tat pattern is not always used because some artists apply tattoos "free hand."

Tattin' *also* **Tackin'** The art of applying tattoos. "Edmundo put two tattoos on Tom today. He has been tattin' all day."

11

VIOLENCE

Weapons

Blade A knife or a sharpened object used as a knife. (Archaic: *mahoska*)

Cap To shoot someone. "Bubba is going to cap that punk if he doesn't quit fooling around."

Heeled To be armed with a weapon. Heeled is mainly used to mean armed with a firearm, but it may be used to mean any weapon. (Archaic: *loaded*)

Keeper Any weapons. Keeper was originally used to mean a knife or knife-like weapon, but has been expanded. (Archaic: *convincer*)

Knucks Any type of brass knuckle or metal finger coverings used for fist fighting. Knucks can be manufactured or, more often, prison made by cutting pieces of pipe to fit over the fingers. Knucks serve two functions when fighting; they protect the fingers and hands and provide a solid, powerful punch.

Nunchucks *also* **Chucks** A martial arts weapon. In prison, nunchucks are made by joining cut sections of broom handles, generally six to twelve inches in length, with leather laces, shoe strings or woven string.

87

Pick An ice pick type weapon. A pick can be a sharpened screwdriver, bedspring or any round, sharpened object. It is normally made with some type of handle. (Archaic: *sticker*)

Pig Sticker A knife or a weapon that is used to stab someone. (Archaic: *toad sticker*)

Pipe *also* **Club** Any weapon that is wielded by a swinging force.

Roscoe A handgun or pistol. (Archaic: *Oscar*)

Shank One of the oldest and most popular terms used to mean a knife. A shank can be a legally manufactured or prison-made knife.
  Any sharpened object used to stab or cut someone is referred to as a shank. (Archaic: *axe*)

Shit Any weapon. (Archaic: *business*)

Shiv A knife or any sharpened object used as a knife.
  The term shiv originated many years ago when the only metal readily available to prisoners was metal spacers or shivs. The spacers were used in cell door hinges to make the cell doors fit properly when closed or to level the metal bunks in the cells. These spacers were obtained by the inmates, sharpened and used as knifes. (Archaic: *chopper*)

Slash Job Self-mutilation of the wrists. Some inmates never adjust to the many continuous hours of confinement. Some of them become "stir crazy" and attempt suicide. Since prison does not offer many ways or opportunities to commit suicide, inmates use whatever they can obtain to cut their veins or slash their wrists.

Sling A belt or a strap with a sharpened belt buckle or metal object attached to one end. Sling is also used to mean any type of flexible weapon wielded by a swinging force, such as a chain or an electrical cord.

Throw Down To threaten a person with a weapon, usually a gun or knife. The actual pointing of the weapon at someone, or its use, is throwing down on him. (Archaic: *put the heat on*)

Zip *also* **Z** A homemade firearm. A zip is generally made of a short length of pipe, usually about four to ten inches long, with an inside diameter the same size as the circumference of the bullet to be fired. The bullet is placed in one end of the pipe while a pointed steel rod is placed in the other end. The pointed end of the rod is used to detonate the bullet and is activated by a sharp blow using the heel of one's hand or a small, solid object. Z's generally have some type of a handle attached to the pipe to hold it stable.

A zip only fires one bullet at a time and the name evolved from the "zip guns" used by city street gangs throughout the United States.

Fighting

Barbeque *also* **Torch 'Em** Burning an inmate by throwing a Molotov cocktail into his cell. This is usually done during a lockdown period and the inmate has no way to get out of his cell quickly. "There is going to be a barbeque tonight."

Blanket Party When a group of inmates throw a blanket over another inmate in a shower or cell area and then proceed to beat or stab him. "That 'fish' with the 'snitch jacket' is begging for a blanket party."

Can also mean a sexual assault of an inmate. (Archaic: *give one the blanket*)

Brown Trout *also* **Slingin' Trout** Throwing body waste on the guards passing the cells. This excrement is referred to as brown trout. The actual throwing of the feces is called slingin' trout.

Usually, slingin' trout occurs during times of unrest or isolated incidents involving one or two inmates. It is not a frequent occurrence.

Drove *also* **Way Drove** Extremely annoyed. (Archaic: *hot in the biscuit, geed up*)

Fire on Someone Used in reference to hitting someone in a fight. Although firing on someone can be accomplished with pipes or clubs, it is primarily used to indicate someone hitting another inmate with his fists.

Flying Lessons Throwing a guard or inmate off of a cell-block tier. This is a more drastic means of dealing with a person who has angered another person or group. It is also a way to deal with an inmate who does not pay his debts or is a "snitch." "I think it is time we gave Joe some flying lessons since he still owes me for the 'weed'."

Going Down *also* **Coming Down** Used to indicate something is happening. "The fight is going down at 7 P.M. in the recreation yard."

Jam A fight. Originally, a jam was a gang fight, but it has been expanded to mean any fight.

Plex *also* **Flex** To become bristled and ready to fight.
Plex may be used in reference to someone expanding their muscles by flexing.

Pluggin' When two inmates are fist fighting, they are said to be pluggin'. (Archaic: *swindle*)

Push Someone's Key To cause someone to become extremely irritated and angry. This is usually accomplished by some form of harassment. (Archaic: *get one's pratt*)

Put on Your Armor Strapping magazines around the torso with strips of sheets to prevent an individual from being stabbed in any confrontative situation.

Rat Packed *also* **Wolf Pack** When three or more inmates attack one. To rat pack someone is generally associated with established gang activity, but it may be used to indicate any occurrence when one or two inmates are attacked by a group of inmates.

Ride Down When a group of inmates or a gang attacks other inmates. A gang can ride down on one inmate or another gang. (Archaic: *take one over the hurdles*)

Scope *also* **Scope It Out** To check out a situation or pay attention to what someone is doing. "There are a lot of cops running over to the chow hall. I think I'll go scope it out."

Scuff Up To fight. The term is primarily used in reference to a fist fight. (Archaic: *jackpot*)

Take Him Down Through There Used in reference to a fight. To take a person down through there is to beat him. This can be done with fists, clubs or other weapons.

Take It in the Blind Refers to inmates settling an argument or fight out of view of prison guards. If two inmates are arguing and prison guards are coming near, other prisoners will warn them to take it in the blind. (Archaic: *put on a slab*)

Wanna Be Imprisonment is an extremely terrifying experience, even for the hardened convict, but especially for the "first timer." Many young men come to prison and are immediately subjected to the violence, sexual harassment and intimidation that are so prevalent within the prison environment. In order to counteract this fear, many young men attempt to emulate the meaner, tougher convicts by acting tough themselves. This type of convict is called a wanna be. This is fear in its most perverse and negative sense and prisons breed this type of behavior.

Intimidation

Bleed To take advantage of or extort someone. "I am going to bleed that new 'fish' for all I can get."

Breathin' My Air Getting too close or invading the privacy of another inmate. "Ted has been breathin' my air and he's beginning to piss me off."

Bulldoggin' *also* **Bulldogger** A coercive variation of the term doggin'. It is a verbal harassment as well as a physical and or verbal intimidation of someone resulting in forcing a person to do something against his will or taking something from him. The prison environment is one in which the bigger and stronger inmates prey on the weaker ones and bulldoggin' is a frequent occurrence. (Archaic: *put the arm on, put the nuts on*)

Call Him on the Carpet Challenge someone to be accountable for his remarks or actions. When someone accuses you of doing something wrong and you call him on the carpet, you are telling him to prove it or stop accusing. "I called him on the carpet when I found out he was putting a bad 'jacket' on me."

Cop Out *also* **Cop To** To admit to something. Originally, cop out was used to admit to crimes a person had committed. But in the prison environment, it is used more to admit to having something—as in: "I think Rick received his new issue of *Hustler* today in the mail but he wouldn't cop out to it."

Cop to sometimes is used to mean cop out—as in: "He copped to having the new magazine."

Coppin' Deuces When an inmate says or does something wrong, then makes excuses or pleas of innocence for what he has done. "He started coppin' deuces when he was caught with my radio."

Dead Wood *also* **Four Cornered** A person who is caught redhanded committing a crime.

Also refers to a person who has absolutely no chance of winning at something. "When he passed me on the last lap, I knew then I couldn't catch him. I knew I was dead wood." (Archaic: *dead pigeon, dead bang*)

Dog Out To treat someone terribly. An inmate who is verbally or physically abused is dogged out.

Another way in which dog out is used is in reference to an inmate's friends excluding him from their activities. (Archaic: *put the chill on*)

Doggin' Constantly verbally harassing someone. This term is derived from the rodeo expression of dogging calves by riding them to the ground. (Archaic: *put the chill on, put the shake on*)

Dump Trucked When a person fails at something because he was nervous and apprehensive about the outcome. Dump trucking is associated with instances in which the person should have been successful.

'Fess Up An old prison expression that means to admit or confess something. "You may as well 'fess up. We know you took the radio." (Archaic: *come clean, dog it*)

Front *also* **Front Off** To accuse someone. "I fronted him off about stealing the radio."
    A person may front someone off by putting him on front street, which is to let other people know what the person is doing.

Get the Bass Out of Your Voice An expression to tell someone to quit acting aggressive or forceful. "You had better get the bass out of your voice or I'll kick your ass."

Jam Up *also* **Jammed Up** *and* **Jam Him Up** To confront someone about a certain issue. "I jammed him up over the money he owes me." Questioning a person about the actions of someone else is another form of confrontation associated with jam up. "Sergeant Smith jammed me up about why you haven't been working. I told him to talk to you about that." (Archaic: *shake*)

Mad Doggin' Non-verbal intimidation. To glare or stare someone down. (Archaic: *bad-eye*)

Nut on Someone To verbally abuse, intimidate, physically challenge or attack a person.

Nut Up To completely lose control of oneself. "George really nutted up when the guard gave him a 'ticket'."
    Nut up is also used in reference to someone laughing hysterically. (Archaic: *blow one's roof, break up*)

Playing Me Too Close This is a phrase used in reference to an inmate who takes advantage of a person's good nature, to the point of making him angry, by constantly teasing or harassing him. This may be done by becoming too personal, "sweating" someone, teasing or harassing. When one inmate tells another he is playing me too close, he is insinuating that he is becoming angry and the other should stop teasing or harassing him.

Pumped Nuts Temporary bravery or aggression. "Fred really kicked his ass. He's had pumped nuts all day."

Sweat To frequently aggravate or harass an inmate about something he may owe you. "I'll probably have to sweat him to get the $10 he owes me." Sweating may be done using force, threats or incessant demanding. (Archaic: *squeeze*)

Wolf Tickets *also* **Wolfin'** *and* **Selling Wolf Tickets** Using threats and intimidation on other inmates. The wolf tickets are the actual threats and the fact that someone is saying these threats is the "selling" of the wolf tickets. If, in fact, you get into a fight over these threats or you are not intimidated in any way, then you have not bought the wolf tickets. If you let these threats frighten you, then you have bought the wolf tickets.

Woofin' A person conveys threats or intimidation to someone. "Bill was woofin' on Tom when he threatened to smack him." (Archaic: *gueril*)

Killing

Hunting License Occasionally certain gang members are assigned to kill someone. This mission is known as a hunting license. "John has a hunting license for the snitch who works in the laundry."

Off To kill someone. "They offed that snitch in the laundry with a zip gun." (Archaic: *knock off*)

Scrag To kill someone. Gang members are sometimes sent on scrag missions which are assignments to kill someone, usually a rival gang member or "snitch." (Archaic: *bang out*)

Take a Person's Wind Killing another inmate. Sometimes a gang will send one of its soldiers on a hit mission to take a rival gang member's wind. (Archaic: *stretch*)

Yoke To kill someone by grasping his throat and choking him.

12

SECURITY & AUTHORITY

Guards

Badge *also* **Shield** A policeman, prison guard or any person in the field of law enforcement who wears a badge or shield.

Big Bull The senior prison officer or the prison guard supervisor on any particular shift.
In some prisons the warden is known as the big bull.

Boss *also* **Boss Man** A prison guard. The term originated in southeastern prisons where work gangs were used to clean along the roadways. The guard in charge of these work gangs was called the boss. The term has since expanded to mean any prison guard or work gang guard. (Archaic: *bum*)

Brown Shirt *also* **Blue Shirt** Terms used for prison guards in reference to the color of their uniform.

Brownie A prison guard named for the brown uniform he or she wears.

Bull One of the oldest terms used to mean a prison guard. Bull originated from the forceful or bullish manner prison guards used to control inmates. (Archaic: *soaker*)

Cage & Key Man A prison guard responsible for a cellhouse or any row of cells in a cellhouse.

Chaser Specific officer assigned to work crews, chain gangs and escape recovery teams.

Copper A facetious term used in reference to a policeman or prison guard. Its levity stems from the manner in which the term was used in the gangster movies of the 1930s and 1940s by movie stars such as James Cagney and Humphrey Bogart.

Dick A term originating from the Dick Tracy comic strip that means detective. A private dick is a private detective. Dick has now expanded to mean any policeman or prison guard. (Archaic: *April fool copper*)

Goon Squad A group or squad of prison guards. Any time there is trouble in the prison, such as gang fighting, a squad of guards is sent to investigate and stop the disturbance.

Goon squad is also used in reference to the guards who perform the searches or shakedowns in the prison. (Archaic: *strong arm squad*)

Hacker *also* **Hack** A prison guard. (Archaic: *mulligan*)

Harness Bull An armed, uniformed prison guard or policeman. (Archaic: *harness cop*)

Heat *also* **Hot** When a person is suspected of committing a particular crime, he is said to be hot. "He has a lot of heat on him for the bank robberies he has been doing."

In prison, heat is used to mean police or prison guards. "Don't light that 'joint' now because the heat is coming."

Another usage for heat is in reference to the consequences for committing a crime. "If you can't stand the heat, don't do the crime."

Herder A prison guard assigned to yard duties where he mingles amongst the prisoners on the prison grounds.

Key Man The guard who unlocks cells. He may not necessarily have actual keys as some cellblocks lock and unlock by means of electrical controls.

Main Man The warden.

The Man Originated many years ago referring to the warden of a prison. The term has since expanded to mean any prison guard, prison official or policeman. In recent years, the term has been used, to a lesser degree, to represent any person holding an authoritative position. (Archaic: *big shot*)

Overseer A prison guard who monitors work gangs or yard activities. The term originated in the slave era of the South and was first used in prison in reference to the guards in charge of the chain gangs that worked outside the prison. It is now used to mean any guard who monitors work crews or yard activities and prison guards who man the gun towers that surround maximum security prisons. (Archaic: *chain-gang Charley, long-line skinner*)

Pig Pig originated during the 1960s hippie movement and referred to a policeman. It has since expanded to encompass police, prison guards and anyone in a position of authority. (Archaic: *dog*)

Screw A prison guard. (Archaic: *roach*)

Shit Helmet Protective head gear worn to protect the prison guards, who work the super-max segregation area of the prison, from the feces and other things thrown at them.

 Protective clothing is only worn during periods of unrest as these incidents are not frequent occurrences.

Trigger A prison guard who carries or has access to a rifle or shotgun. Trigger is generally used to indicate the prison guards manning the gun towers. (Archaic: *turret-man*)

Turnkey *also* **Key** *and* **Keys** A name given to prison guards in reference to the large ring of keys they carry and the loud, jingling sound they make.

 When inmates gather to do something illegal, they assign one inmate to be a lookout. This lookout not only watches for the guards but listens for the clanging sound of the keys as well. "Stop doing that tattoo, the turnkey is coming." (Archaic: *spindle*)

Twister A prison guard assigned to a cellhouse. The term "twister" is derived from the large ring of keys the officer uses to lock and unlock the cells and security doors throughout the prison.

Areas & Searches

Black Maria A prison van used for transporting prisoners.

Briefing Room An area or room designated for apprising prison guards of their shift instructions and providing other information.

Checkpoint Certain areas throughout maximum and most medium security prisons manned by prison guards to monitor inmate traffic. At these checkpoints prisoners may be searched, checked with a metal detector and required to show a pass or prison identification card in order to pass through. Checkpoints are strategically located so inmates are required to pass through them no matter where they go.

Frisk An old term used to mean a "pat-down" search of an inmate. This is accomplished by having the inmate remove the contents of his pockets. The guard then pats the prisoner's body looking for contraband. (Archaic: *prowl*)

Gun Tower *also* **Guard Tower** *and* **Tower** All maximum and many medium security prisons have a high wall or fence surrounding the prison grounds. Strategically spaced along these fences are lofty structures with shed-like enclosures at the top. These enclosures are manned by armed prison guards and used as observation points. These structures are known as guard towers, gun towers or simply towers.

Hit Your House Occasionally, prison guards will conduct random searches or shakedowns of inmates' cells or living areas looking for weapons, drugs or other contraband. This type of search is referred to as hitting your house. (Archaic: *toss*)

Mechanical Stool Pigeon *also* **Mechanical Stoolie** A walk-through metal detector. (Archaic: *snitcher*)

Patdown *also* **Pat Search** A means of search whereby the prison guards pat the inmate's body and legs with their hands while looking for weapons or contraband. (Archaic: *rubdown*)

Shakedown A prison term meaning search. A shakedown may be performed on one's person, cell or living area, clothing or other personal property. (Archaic: *general*)

Skin Frisk An old term used to mean a strip search of an inmate. This is accomplished by having the prisoner remove all his clothing. The clothing is thoroughly checked as is each orifice of the inmate's body.

Strip Search *also* **Strip You Out** In all prisons, inmates are constantly being searched; as they enter and leave their work assignments or housing units, pass through checkpoints or re-enter the prison from visitation. Normally, this search consists of a patdown and the emptying of pockets. On some occasions, however, when the staff is looking for weapons, drugs or other contraband, it is necessary to conduct a more thorough search. This is done by strip searching the inmate whereby the person is forced to remove all his clothing. Each piece of clothing is thoroughly inspected as is each orifice of the body. (Archaic: *strip frisk*)

Wall Box A gun tower that is located on top of the wall that surrounds some prisons. Most maximum security prisons are surrounded by a concrete wall ranging from 25 to 40 feet in height. Strategically placed along the top of the wall are box-like enclosures used for observation. These enclosures are manned by armed guards.

Yard Office A security office for officers of the prison guards. This office is used for investigations and yard operations.

Crimes & Rioting

Air Mail Garbage or things thrown from windows of cellhouses or cells onto prison guards. This usually happens during riots or periods of unrest and is usually thrown from the upper tiers of cells or upper windows of cellhouses.

Bingo A prison riot. (Archaic: *kick over*)

B.O.L. Stands for "Be on the lookout" and is used when inmates are doing illegal activities. Someone is posted to keep watch for the guards. "Don't worry, John is on the B.O.L."

Rockin' A prison riot. When prisoners riot, it is said the joint is rockin'. (Archaic: *kick-up*)

Tweezers Tools inmates use to break into cells and lockers in prison. Prison cells often get burglarized and robbed just as homes do.

13

PAROLE & RECORDS

Parole

The Board The parole board. Can also mean the pardon board. Parole boards are a separate entity from the department of corrections and their powers vary greatly from one state to another. In many states they are merely a rubber stamp which releases inmates who have had no major problems serving their time. For instance, if an inmate were sentenced to 10 years and were eligible for parole in 5 years, the board would review his file and if there were no problems, he would automatically get released.

In other states the board has much more power and in reality serves as a second court trial. If they feel the crime was serious or the person did not get enough time, they will not grant parole regardless of your prison record.

Paper When an inmate is granted parole, he is referred to as being on paper. Paper literally means parole or probation and is derived from the parole papers containing the rules and conditions of the parole the inmate must sign before being granted parole. "He made paper today."

Tail A term meaning parole. "He has a six month tail." This means he has to serve six months on parole. A tail may be referred to as strict, supervised, unsupervised or obligatory. The strict and supervised tails have numerous rules and requirements the parolee must obey, like weekly

101

meetings with a parole officer, counseling, and random urinalysis tests to detect alcohol or drugs. The unsupervised and obligatory tails have few rules and requirements. "I'm sure glad I made parole but I sure have a long tail." (Archaic: *owe time*)

Violate To break the conditions of "parole." (Archaic: *kick parole*)

Records

Bad Paper Reports or legal documents which reflect something negative about an inmate. "Be careful of Neal, I have seen some bad paper on him."

Jacket A person's Department of Corrections record file. In this file is kept every piece of information about the inmate amassed throughout his prison sentence, whether it is positive or negative. Inmates are continually trying to get positive documentation placed in their jackets with the intention of influencing the parole board.

Another way in which jacket is used is the invisible jacket or label placed on someone for a particular character triat. An informant or "snitch" has a "snitch jacket" placed on him. This information will follow the individual from one institution to another and even to other states via the "inmate grapevine." Other jackets placed on inmates are: homosexual, liar, thief and drug user. Due to the excessive amount of gossip and rumor in prison, a false jacket is often placed on someone.

A person's criminal history is sometimes referred to as his jacket. "We learned from his jacket he has been known to carry a gun."

Kite *also* **Flyin' a Kite** *and* **Shoot a Kite** Any type of written correspondence used in prison. A kite can be a letter, memo, note or an official inmate request form. Sending a kite to someone is referred to as shoot him a kite or fly a kite to him. (Archaic: *tab*)

Package *also* **Parole Package** Positive documentation, verifying the ways an inmate is trying to better himself. This paperwork is amassed with the intention of influencing the parole board.

Pedigree An inmate's criminal history, such as arrest record, number and types of convictions, and number of times in prison.

Pencil Whip *also* **Paper Whip** Inmates who file many lawsuits or grievances are referred to as pencil whipping the system. Although some of these lawsuits or grievances are won, the institution generally wins in the end.

Programming The programs an inmate utilizes, either for self-help or to influence the parole board.

Rap Sheet *also* **Sheet** A person's criminal history. Every time a person is arrested for a crime, a record of that arrest along with the disposition or results of the arrest is kept on file with the Federal Bureau of Investigation (F.B.I.) in Washington, D.C. (Archaic: *pedigree*)

Ticket *also* **Write-Up** When an inmate is found in violation of prison rules, he is given a ticket or write-up. This is a standard disciplinary form stating the offense, time and day the infraction occurred and disposition procedures. Each prison has different classifications of violations with respect to severity, and the penalties will vary with these different categories.

14

DEATH IN PRISON

Air Dance *also* **Dance** Inmates executed by hanging are said to have done the air dance.

Back Gate Exit A term used to indicate an inmate dying in prison. Since most prison cemeteries are located behind the prison or out the back gate, an inmate who dies in prison is said to have received a back gate exit.

Not all prisons have cemeteries. Most always the inmate cemetery for a state will be located at the oldest and or largest maximum security institution of that state. If an inmate dies at some other prison that does not have its own cemetery, and is not claimed by anyone, the body will be sent to the inmate cemetery at the maximum security prison for burial.

Barbecue Stool *also* **Barbecue** A prison electric chair used for executing inmates.

Blood Box *also* **Butcher Wagon** An ambulance.

Bone Box A hearse.

Capun Refers to capital punishment and is used to indicate someone receiving the death penalty.

Chamber A prison gas chamber used for executing inmates.

Check Out An inmate who commits suicide in prison.

Croaker A prison doctor. (Archaic: *butcher, pill roller*)

D.C. *also* **C.C.** Prisons that are equipped for execution have a separate building or area that houses the execution chamber. Also in this building is a security cell where the inmate is kept just prior to his execution, usually the 24-hour period prior to his scheduled execution time. This cell is called the "death cell" or "condemned cell" and is commonly known as the "D.C." or the "C.C."

Dutch Act *also* **Dutch Route** Committing suicide in prison.

Electric Cure To be electrocuted.

Get the Works Receive the death penalty. "John got the works for killing those people."

Give a Permanent Wave To electrocute someone.

Halter A hangman's noose. (Archaic: *antiquated*)

Hot Squat *also* **Hot Seat** The electric chair.

Last Waltz A condemned prisoner's walk from the death cell to the execution chamber at the time of his execution.

Lifeboat When an inmate who has been sentenced to death gets his death sentence overturned or commuted to a life sentence, it is said that he got a "lifeboat."

Old Smokey Electric chair in an execution chamber.

Pinchers Up When a person dies he is said to be pinchers up. (Archaic: *kick off*)

Pine Box Release *also* **Pine Box Parole** When an inmate dies in prison. (Archaic: *back gate commute*)

Sizzle Seat An electric chair.

Sky Pilot A prison chaplain. (Archaic: *sinhound, holy Joe*)

Smogged When an inmate is executed in a gas chamber, it is said that he was smogged.

Squat The electric chair or electrocution.

Yoke To cut someone's throat from behind. The prison environment is an extremely dangerous one with stabbings and killings happening often. One of the more commonly used methods of attacking and killing someone is to sneak up behind him and cut his throat with a knife.

15

GETTING OUT

Release

Abscond To escape any type of police custody, whether it is from prison, a work release center, a half-way house, or to leave while on parole.

Cop a Heel *also* **Cop a Moke** To escape from prison.

Crash *also* **Crash Out** Escape.

Cut Loose Released from prison. (Archaic: *back in circulation*)

Free World *also* **Free Side** Anything outside the confines of an institution. (Archaic: *the outside*)

Hallelujah Chorus When an inmate is released from prison, he is referred to as singing the hallelujah chorus.
 Also can be used to mean an inmate who dies while in prison.

Hit the Streets To be released from prison. (Archaic: *kick out*)

In the Wind When an inmate has left prison on parole or sentence expiration, he is referred to as being in the wind. (Archaic: *spring*)

Kill a Number *also* **Number** *and* **Parole to Next Number** To complete a prison sentence. Many inmates have been to prison several times for differing offenses. Even though an inmate is assigned only one D.O.C. or identification number within a particular prison system, each sentence he serves is referred to as another number. Each state varies in its method of recording the number of times a person goes to prison, but most use an A, B, C or 1, 2, 3 following the D.O.C. number—as in: A person with a number of 12345-D or 12345-4 has been in prison four times.

To kill a number is also used in reference to consecutive prison sentences whereby an inmate must complete or kill one number before serving the next sentence. Since this is often accomplished through the parole system, it is known as paroling to the next number. (Archaic: *all of it*)

Max Out *also* **Max a Number** Refers to an inmate who serves his entire prison sentence before being released. This means the inmate was not credited with any "good time." (Archaic: *works*)

On the Ground When an inmate is released from prison it is said he is on the ground or back on the ground.

Raise To get out of prison. (Archaic: *leave one the bucket*)

Streets Life outside the prison. The streets is an expression used extensively throughout prison to refer to anything or anyone outside prison life. "He will be on the streets again if he makes parole." (Archaic: *the bricks*)

Escape

Fence Cons Inmates who have escaped or attempted to escape.

Goin' Over the Wall This is an escape expression originating in maximum security prisons that are surrounded by concrete or brick walls. (Archaic: *hit the wall, hit the hump*)

Jackrabbit Parole Escape. (Archaic: *bush parole*)

Make Bush *also* **Bush Patrol** To escape from prison.

Mole An inmate who escapes by digging his way out of the prison. (Archaic: *hole*)

Rabbit Blood The desire to run or escape. Many people who have lost their freedom due to incarceration have contemplated regaining this freedom by means of escape. This trait is known as rabbit blood. The more a person attempts to escape, the more rabbit blood he has. (Archaic: *have go-go in one's eyes*)

Sweatin' the Fence Inmates who contemplate or aspire to escape are referred to as sweatin' the fence. (Archaic: *looking for an out*)

Takin' a Flier A seldom used expression meaning to escape from prison. (Archaic: *blow, beat*)

Tunnel Rat *also* **To Tunnel** In maximum security prisons, some inmates prefer the tunnel method of escape because the security is so great and the walls are too high to contemplate any other way. To escape in this manner is to tunnel and the escaping inmates are known as tunnel rats. (Archaic: *dig a hole*)

INDEX

111